Bridal Bouquets

*Tips to Design
Your Own Wedding Flowers*

VON D. GALT

Copyright © 2015 Von D. Galt

All rights reserved. This book, or ebook, or parts thereof may not be reproduced in any form, stored in a retrieval system, or transmitted in any form by any means – electronic, mechanical, photocopy, recording, or otherwise – without prior written consent and permission of the author except in the case of brief quotations in articles and reviews as provided by the United States of America copyright law.

While the author has made every effort to provide accurate information at the time of publication, neither the publisher nor the author assumes responsibilities for errors or for changes that occur after publication.

Please, consider requesting that your local library branch purchase a copy of this volume.

ISBN-13:978-1516946563

www.VonGaltFlowers.com

Cover designed by Von D. Galt

Edited by Evan Galt

Photography by Von D. Galt

Dedicated to my family,
my friends,
and my husband, Evan
for their continued support

CONTENTS

Introduction i
Chapter 1 Bouquets 1
Chapter 2 Boutonnieres and Corsages 56
Chapter 3 Altar Arrangements 61
Chapter 4 Centerpieces 66
Chapter 5 Planning Your Flowers 69
    Guest List 70
    Guest and Flowers Checklist 71
    Budget and Ordering 72
    Suggested Amounts for the Pre-Order 74
    Design 77
    Labor 77
    Storage 78
    Conditioning Your Flowers 80
    Delivery 81
    Set-up 83
Chapter 6 Care Instructions For Flowers 85
Chapter 7 Wedding Day Timeline 88
Chapter 8 Salutations 93
About the Author 95
Index 96

Introduction

When you look at wedding photos, do you wonder what makes some weddings look so much more elegant than others? Do you wonder what they could have done to add to the ambiance?

If so, then the answer is adding more flowers to the decorations. The wedding mood can be set by decorating the altar and reception room with luxurious flowers. This is what your photographer takes photos of before the wedding ceremony begins. It is what guests walk through when they enter the venue and look around while they patiently wait.

When the ceremony begins, the guests stand up and are amazed at how wonderful the wedding party is fashioned. The corsages and boutonnieres on them are a perfect accent to their well-tailored outfits.

The grand entrance is showcased by the bride, who holds a bouquet that is an artistic expression unique to her and that complements her lovely dress. This is what you want, and I will help you get there.

Now, before making any of these bouquets that follows the introduction, I suggest reading through the "Planning Your Flowers" section first. If you are doing your own flowers, this section will explain the need to do a dry run and pre-plan your flowers. That way you get what you desire without headache.

1
Bouquets

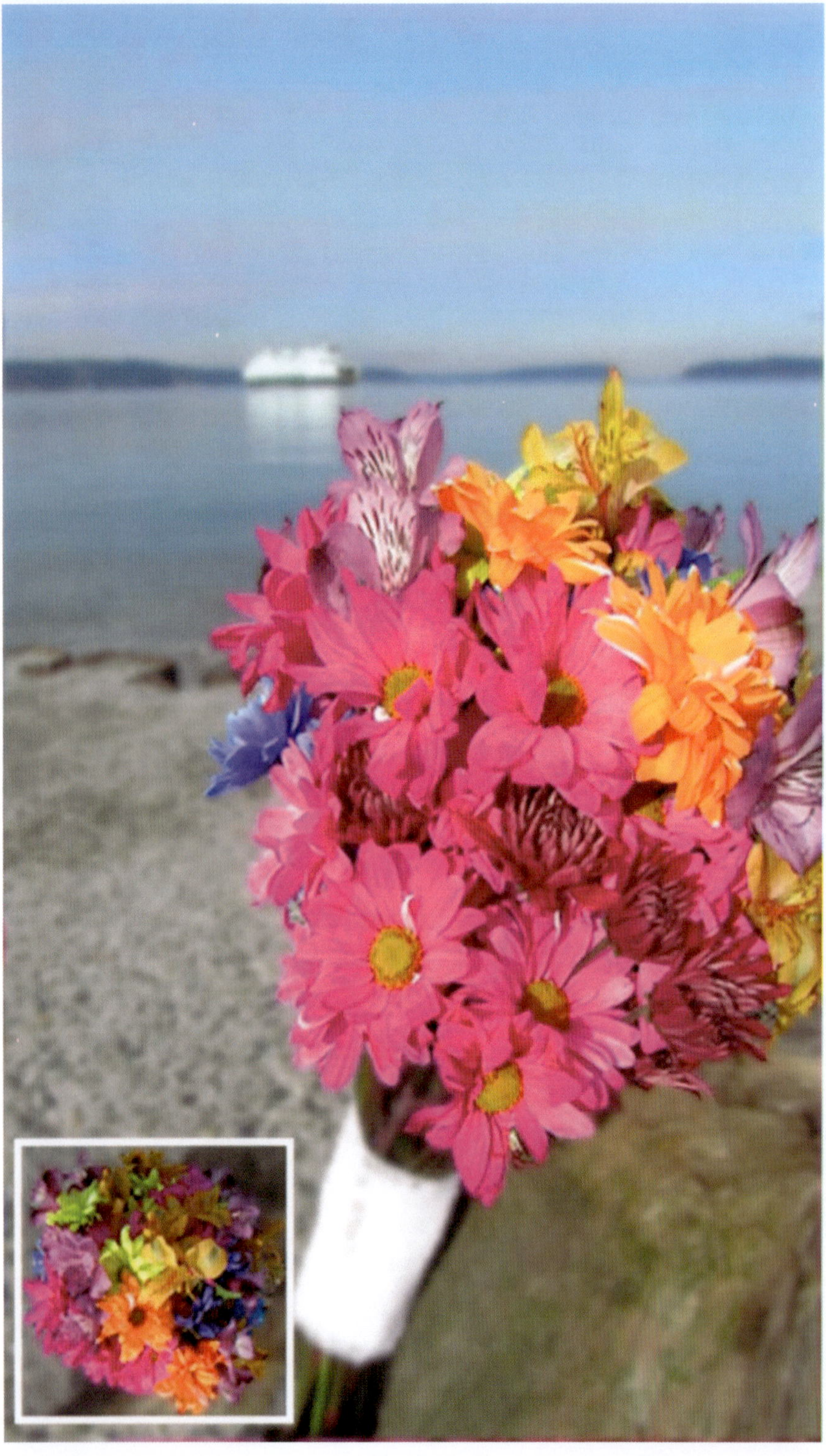

Happy Delights Bouquet

This bouquet pops with enthusiasm in remembrance of childhood.

MATERIALS:

8-12 colorful dyed daisies, 4-6 maroon mums, 4-6 purple alstromeri, 4-6 yellow alstromeri, floral tape, white country lace ribbon, white satin ribbon, corsage pins, and pruning shears.

INSTRUCTIONS:

1. Prep your flowers by reading the "Condition Your Flowers" section of this book.
2. Gather a couple of daisies with one hand like you are holding a bouquet. With your other hand, insert other flowers one at a time in different spots. Make sure to arrange outwards and downwards into a round, ball pattern. Try not to have flowers stick too far out.
3. When you have a basic shape, secure it by wrapping floral tape around it with your free hand.
4. Continue inserting more flowers, but adjust some flowers so new ones fit. Add floral tape as you go to secure the design. Make sure to work the flowers downward to create a ball shape. Secure the final look with floral tape.
5. SAFETY ALERT: Before using the pruning shears to cut the stems to the desired length, pay attention to where your fingers are. Cut away from your fingers and nowhere close to them.
6. Wrap the white satin ribbon around the stem and secure the end of the ribbon by inserting 2-3 pins downward. Repeat with the white country lace ribbon.

See "Care Instructions" section for details on proper care.

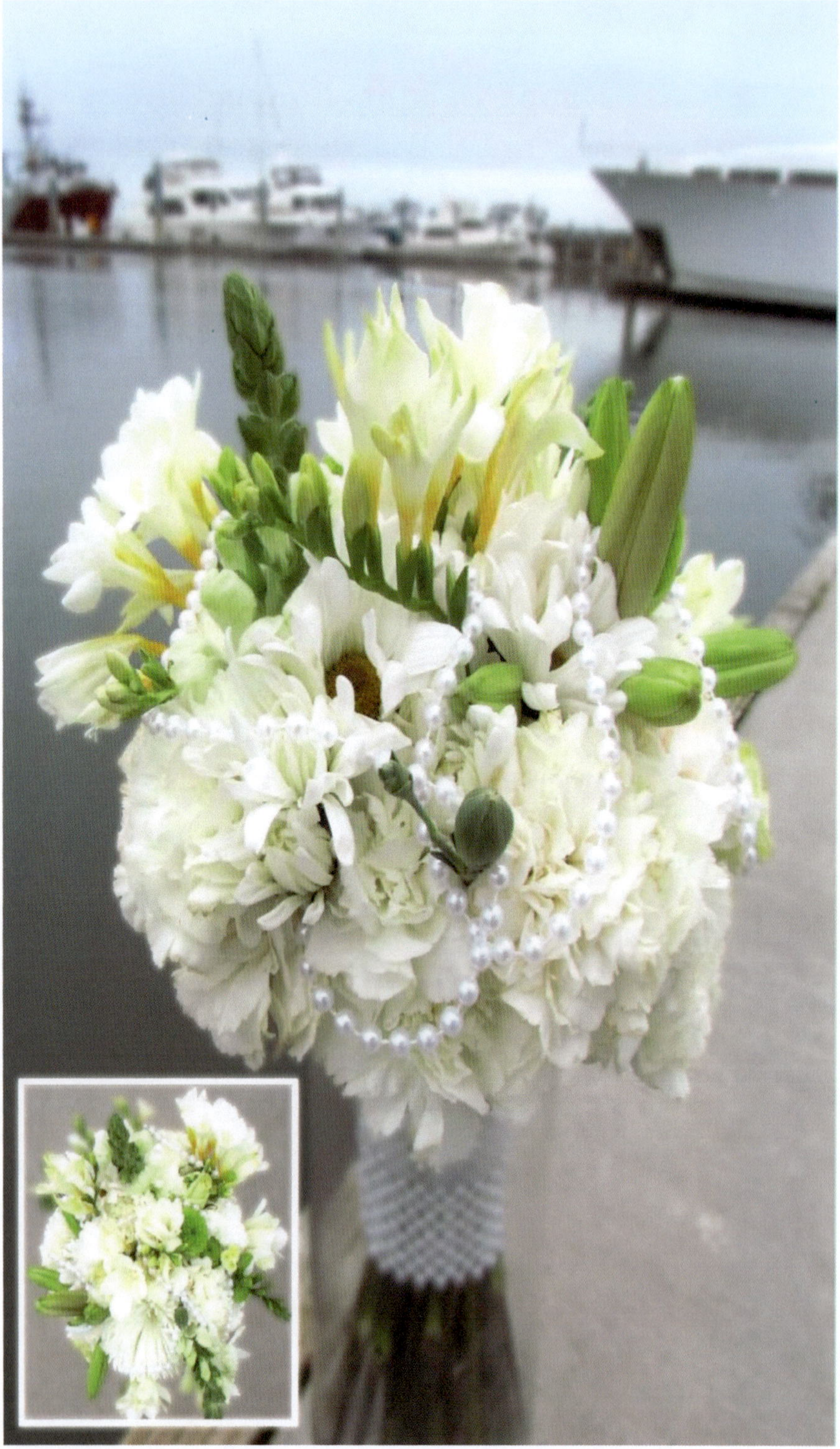

Pearly White Bouquet

This white bouquet is also wearing pearls!

MATERIALS:

6-8 white carnations, 4-6 white daisies, 4 white mums. 4-6 white freesias, 2-3 bloomed white lilies, floral tape, white satin ribbon, pearl wrist corsage, pearl strands, corsage pins, and pruning shears.

INSTRUCTIONS:

1. Prep your flowers by reading the "Condition Your Flowers" section of this book.
2. Gather a lily and a couple of the other flowers with one hand like you are holding a bouquet. With your other hand, insert other flowers one at a time where desired. Make sure to arrange outwards and downwards into a round, ball pattern. Try not to have flowers stick too far out. Reserve the freesias for later.
3. Wrap the basic shape with floral tape around it using your free hand. Continue inserting more flowers, but adjust some flowers so new ones fit. Add freesias where desired. Secure the final look by wrapping floral tape around it.
4. SAFETY ALERT: Before using the pruning shears to cut the stems to the desired length, pay attention to where your fingers are. Cut away from your fingers and nowhere close to them.
5. Wrap the ribbon around the stem and secure the end of the ribbon by inserting 2-3 pins downward. Remove the pearl band from the wrist corsage and cover the bouquet with it, then lace the pearl strands around the bouquet.

See "Care Instructions" section for details on proper care.

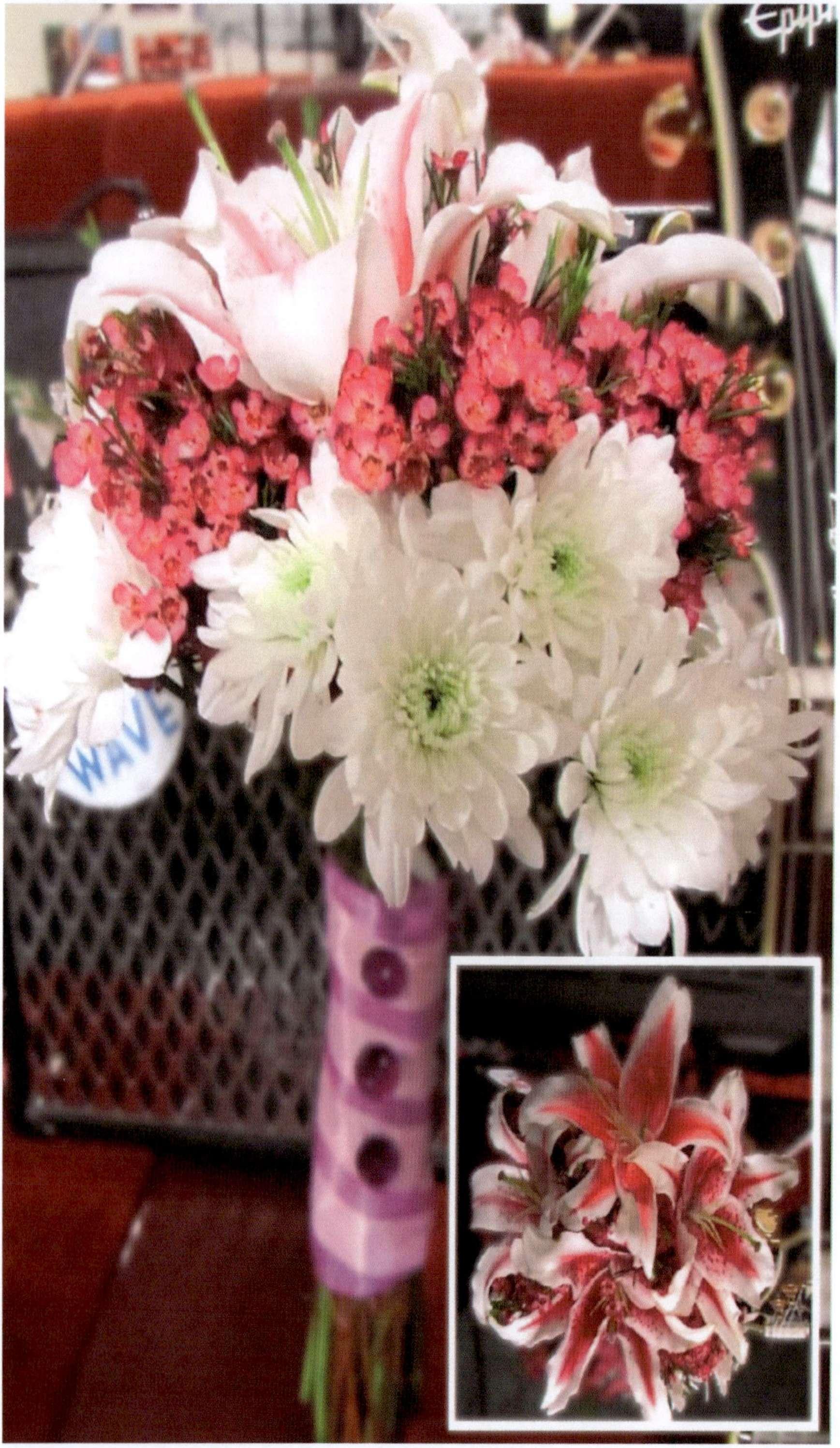
WAVE

Three Tiers Bouquet

You can see all three layers
of beauty in this creation.

MATERIALS:

6-8 white daisy poms, 6-8 pink wax flowers, 3-4 pink oriental lilies, lavender satin ribbon, thin purple ribbon, burgundy rhinestones, hot-glue gun, corsage pins, and pruning shears.

INSTRUCTIONS:

1. Prep your flowers by reading the "Condition Your Flowers" section of this book.
2. Gather a couple of wax flowers with one hand like you are holding a bouquet. With your other hand, insert lilies one at a time in different spots on the top. Gather the daisies around the sides. Make sure to arrange outwards and downwards into a round, ball pattern. When you have a basic shape, secure it by wrapping floral tape around it with your free hand.
3. When the final look is achieved, secure with floral tape.
4. SAFETY ALERT: Before using the pruning shears to cut the stems to the desired length, pay attention to where your fingers are. Cut away from your fingers and nowhere close to them.
5. Wrap the satin ribbon around the stem and secure the end of the ribbon by inserting 2-3 pins downward. Wrap thin ribbon around and secure with pins. Lastly, hot-glue gun the rhinestones along the ribbon.

See "Care Instructions" section for details on proper care.

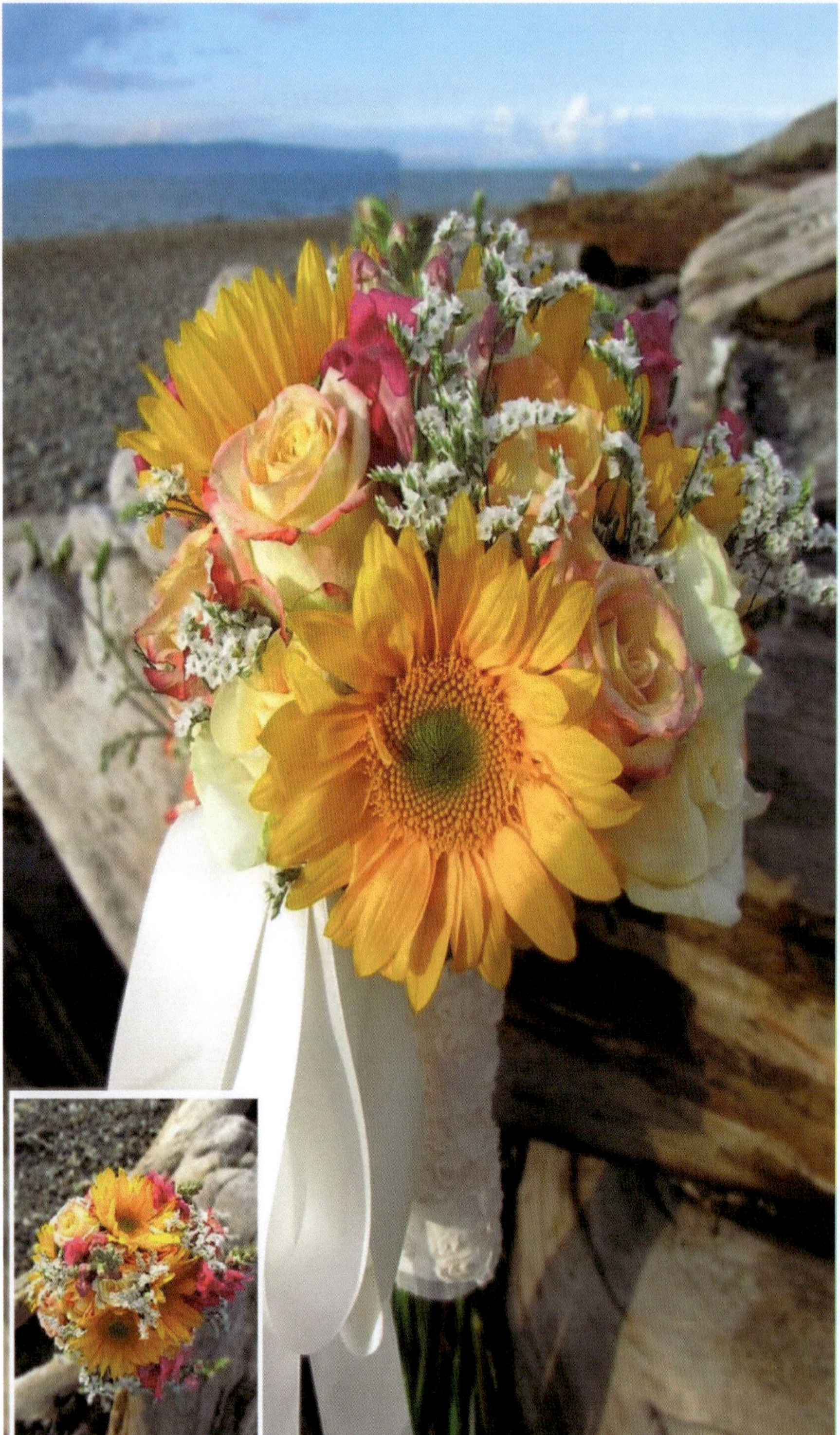

Sunflower and Friends Bouquet

The joy of summer is captured with sunflowers and a mix of other summer flowers in this bouquet.

MATERIALS:

6-8 white static, 8-12 yellow roses, 8-12 white roses, 6-8 red stock flowers, 3-4 sunflowers, ivory lace ribbon, ivory bow, corsage pins, and pruning shears.

INSTRUCTIONS:

1. Prep your flowers by reading the "Condition Your Flowers" section of this book.
2. Gather a couple of stock and static flowers with one hand like you are holding a bouquet. With your other hand, insert roses one at a time in different spots on the top. Reserve the sunflowers for later. Make sure to arrange outwards and downwards into a round, ball pattern. When you have a basic shape, secure it by wrapping floral tape around it with your free hand.
3. Continue inserting more flowers. Inset sunflowers where desires. Secure the final look with floral tape.
4. SAFETY ALERT: Before using the pruning shears to cut the stems to the desired length, pay attention to where your fingers are. Cut away from your fingers and nowhere close to them.
5. Wrap the lace ribbon around the stem and secure the end of the ribbon by inserting 2-3 pins downward. Tie the bow to the base of the bouquet.

See "Care Instructions" section for details on proper care.

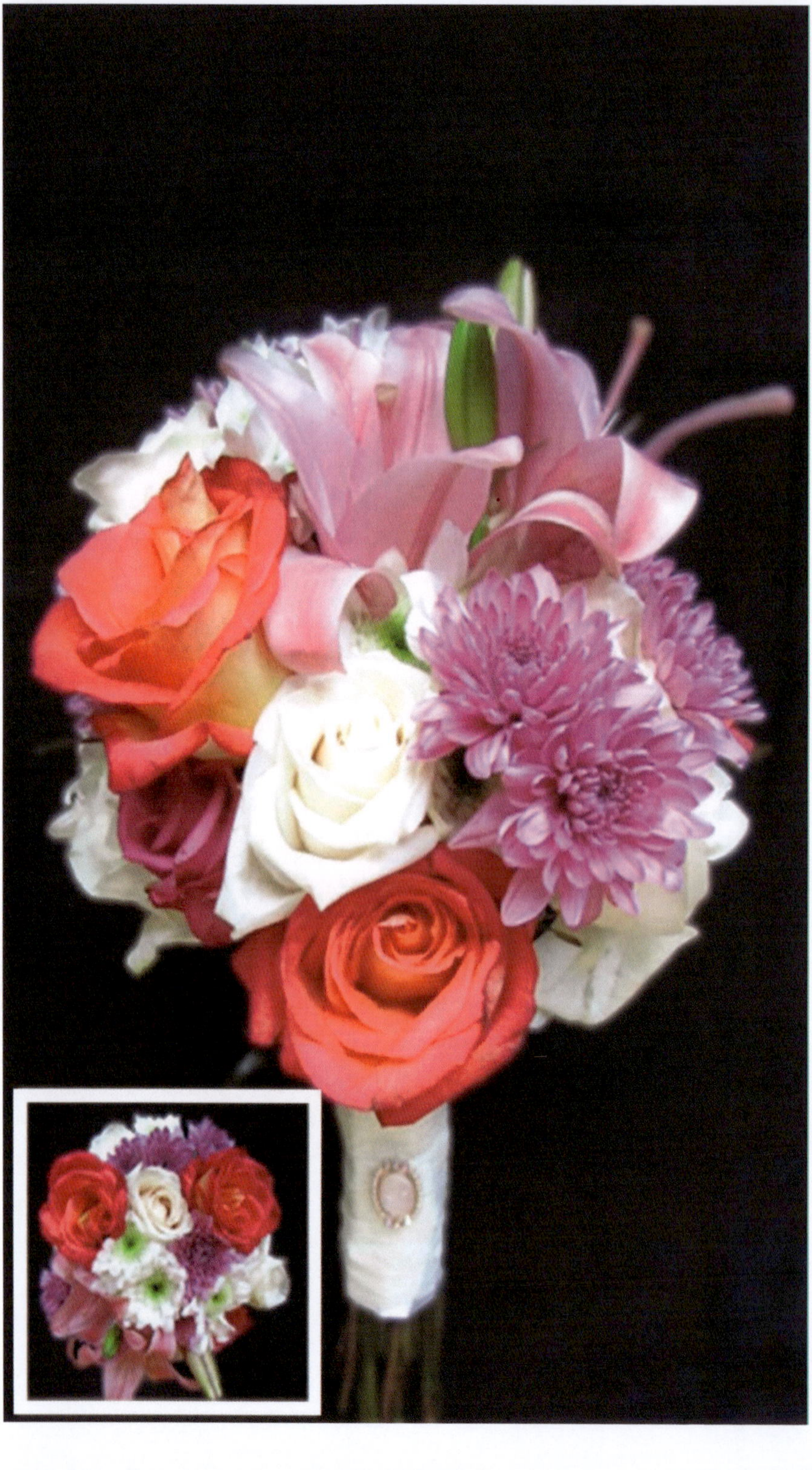

First Crush Bouquet

The hues of pink, lavender, and ivory of these everyday flowers are reminiscent of your first crush.

MATERIALS:

8-12 ivory roses, -12 bi-color pink roses, 6-8 purple roses, 6-8 purple mums, 3-4 pink Asiatic lilies, ivory lace ribbon, brooch, corsage pins, and pruning shears.

INSTRUCTIONS:

1. Prep your flowers by reading the "Condition Your Flowers" section of this book.
2. Gather a couple of roses with one hand like you are holding a bouquet. With your other hand, insert other flowers one at a time in different spots. Make sure to arrange outwards and downwards into a round, ball pattern. When you have a basic shape, secure it by wrapping floral tape around it with your free hand.
3. Continue inserting more flowers, and then gather more roses around the base of the bouquet. Secure the final look with floral tape.
4. SAFETY ALERT: Before using the pruning shears to cut the stems to the desired length, pay attention to where your fingers are. Cut away from your fingers and nowhere close to them.
5. Wrap the ribbon around the stem and secure the end of the ribbon by inserting 2-3 pins downward and pins along the back. Pin brooch on the front of the ribbon.

See "Care Instructions" section for details on proper care.

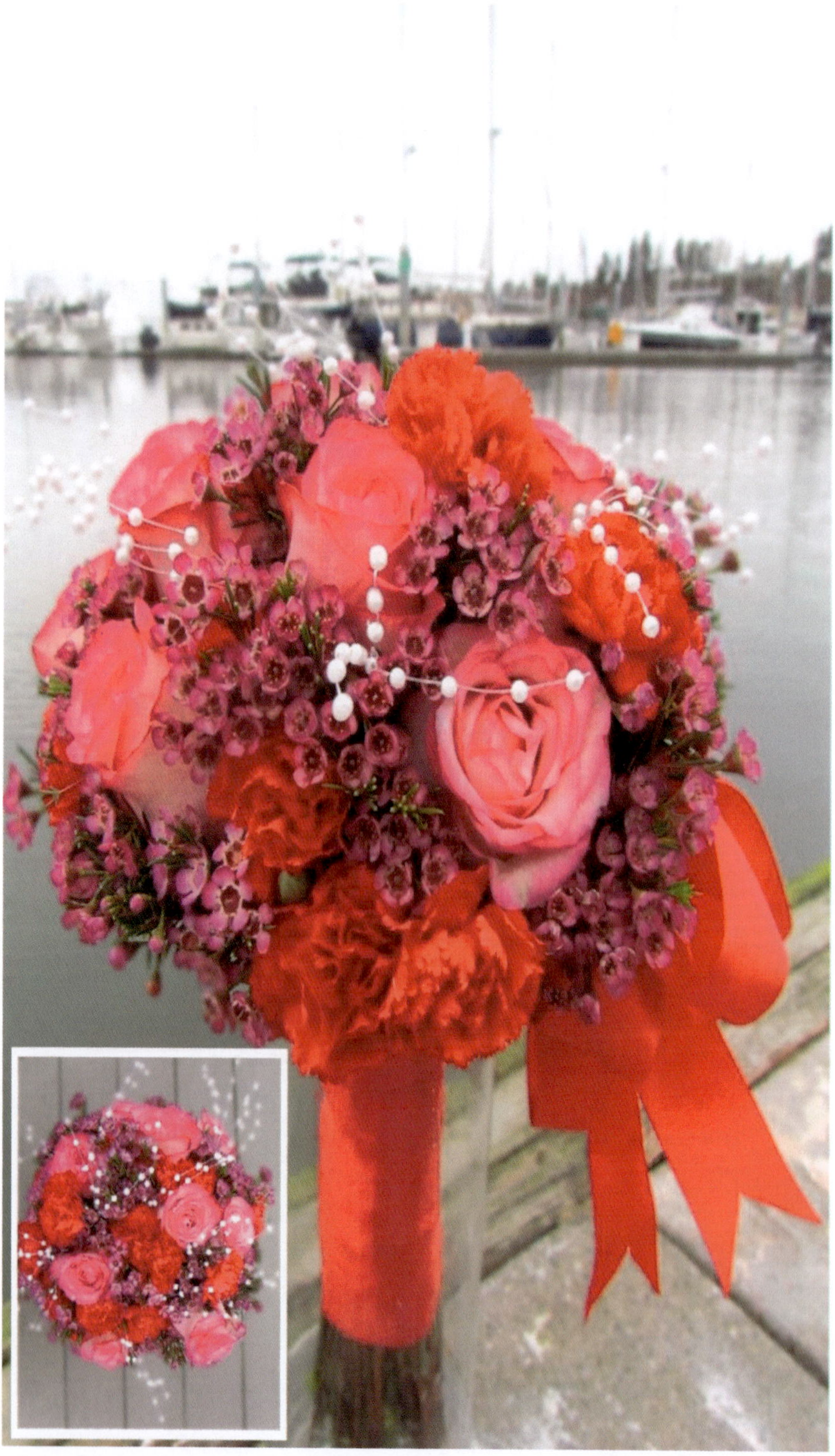

Romance of the Sea Bouquet

The sea was the inspiration for this blend of red and purple flowers.

MATERIALS:

8-12 purple wax flowers, 8-12 red carnations, 8-12 pink roses, pearl shoots, red satin ribbon, red bow, corsage pins, and pruning shears.

INSTRUCTIONS:

1. Prep your flowers by reading the "Condition Your Flowers" section of this book.
2. Gather a couple of wax flowers with one hand like you are holding a bouquet. With your other hand, insert other flowers one at a time in different spots. Make sure to arrange outwards and downwards into a round, ball pattern. Wrap the basic shape with floral tape around it using your free hand.
3. Continue inserting more flowers. Insert the pearl shoots into the bouquet where desired. Add the bow to the side of the bouquet. Secure the final look with floral tape.
4. SAFETY ALERT: Before using the pruning shears to cut the stems to the desired length, pay attention to where your fingers are. Cut away from your fingers and nowhere close to them.
5. Wrap the satin ribbon around the stem and secure the end of the ribbon by inserting 2-3 pins downward and pins along the back.

See "Care Instructions" section for details on proper care.

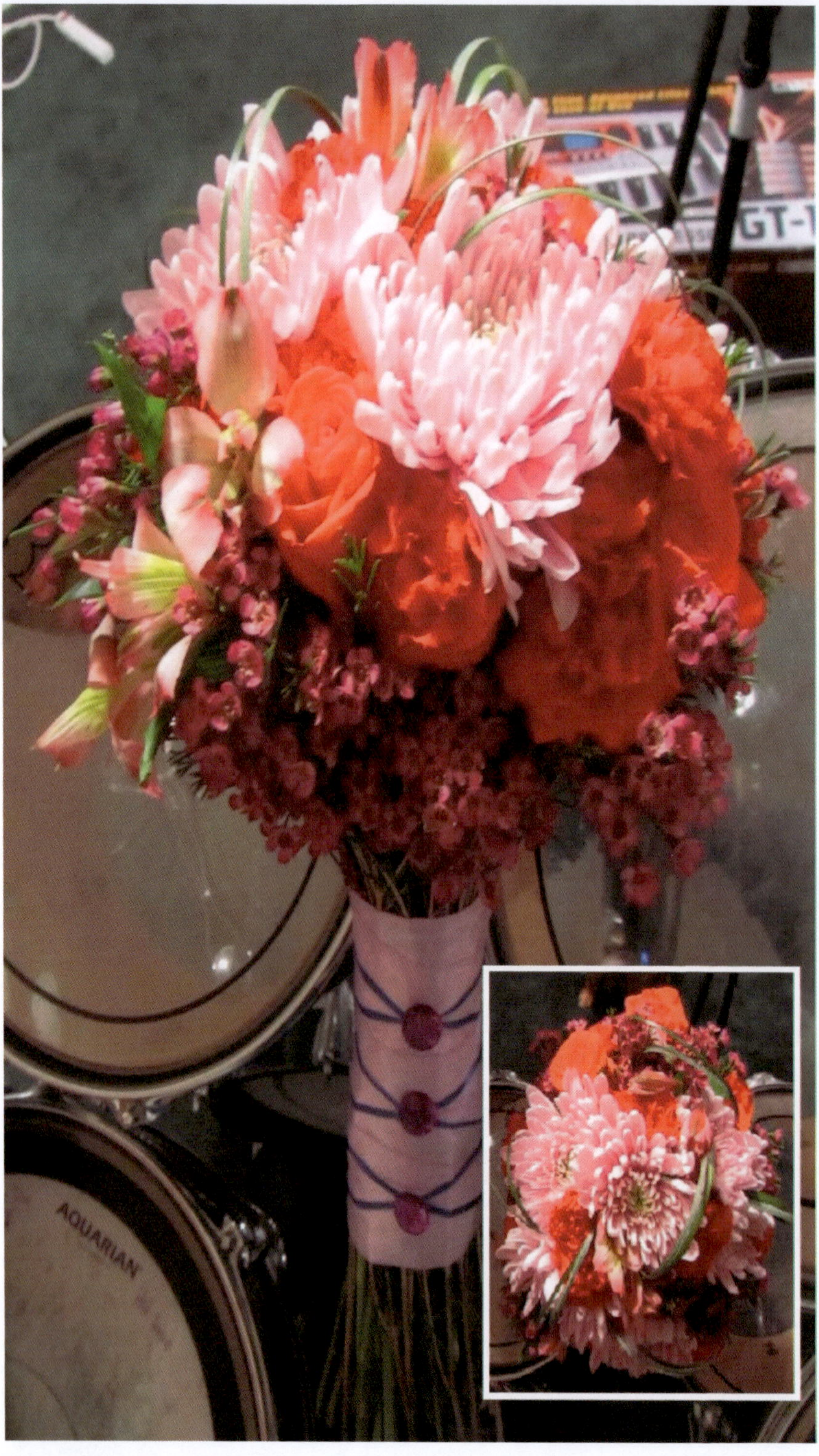
AQUARIAN

Rock of Love Bouquet

This bouquet just rocks!

MATERIALS:

4-6 dark pink wax flowers, 2-4 red alstromeri, 4-6 pink poms, 4-6 red carnations, 6-8 red roses, 2-3 strands of tall grass, lavender satin ribbon, thin blue ribbon, red buttons, corsage pins, hot-glue gun, and pruning shears.

INSTRUCTIONS:

1. Prep your flowers by reading the "Condition Your Flowers" section of this book.
2. Gather a couple of wax flowers with one hand like you are holding a bouquet. With your other hand, insert other flowers one at a time. Make sure to arrange outwards and downwards into a round, ball pattern. Secure the basic shape by wrapping floral tape around it with your free hand. Reserve the grass.
3. Continue inserting more flowers. Secure the final look with floral tape around it. Fold the grass in half and insert the ends into the bouquet where desired.
4. SAFETY ALERT: Before using the pruning shears to cut the stems to the desired length, pay attention to where your fingers are. Cut away from your fingers and nowhere close to them.
5. Wrap the satin ribbon around the stem and secure the end of the ribbon by inserting 2-3 pins downward. Wrap the thin ribbon around it in a criss-cross design and pin the intersections as you go, then pin the end of the ribbon back. Hot glue the buttons on top of the intersections.

See "Care Instructions" section for details on proper care.

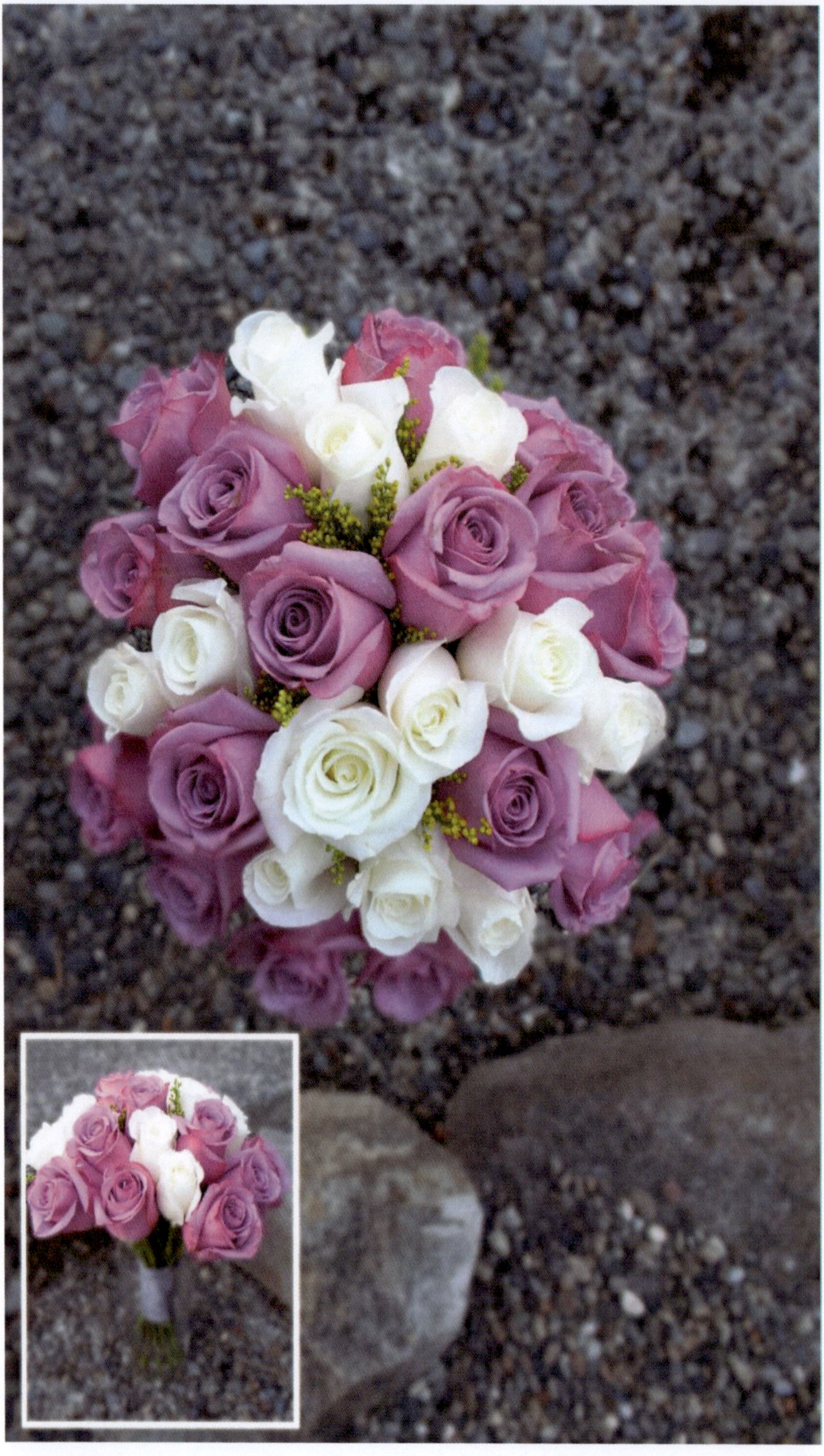

Purple and Ivory Roses Bouquet

This bouquet fuses two popular colors together with semi-closed roses.

MATERIALS:

12-18 ivory roses, 12-18 purple roses, floral tape, ivory satin ribbon, corsage pins, and pruning shears.

INSTRUCTIONS:

1. Prep your flowers by reading the "Condition Your Flowers" section of this book.
2. Gather a couple of ivory and purple roses with one hand like you are holding a bouquet. With your other hand, insert other roses one at a time in different spots. Make sure to arrange outwards and downwards into a round, ball pattern. Try not to have flowers stick too far out.
3. When you have a basic shape, secure it by wrapping floral tape around it with your free hand.
4. Continue inserting more flowers, but adjust some flowers so new ones fit. Add floral tape as you go to secure the design. Make sure to work the flowers downward to create a ball shape. Secure the final look with floral tape.
5. SAFETY ALERT: Before using the pruning shears to cut the stems to the desired length, pay attention to where your fingers are. Cut away from your fingers and nowhere close to them.
6. Wrap the ivory satin ribbon around the stem and secure the end of the ribbon by inserting 2-3 pins downward.

See "Care Instructions" section for details on proper care.

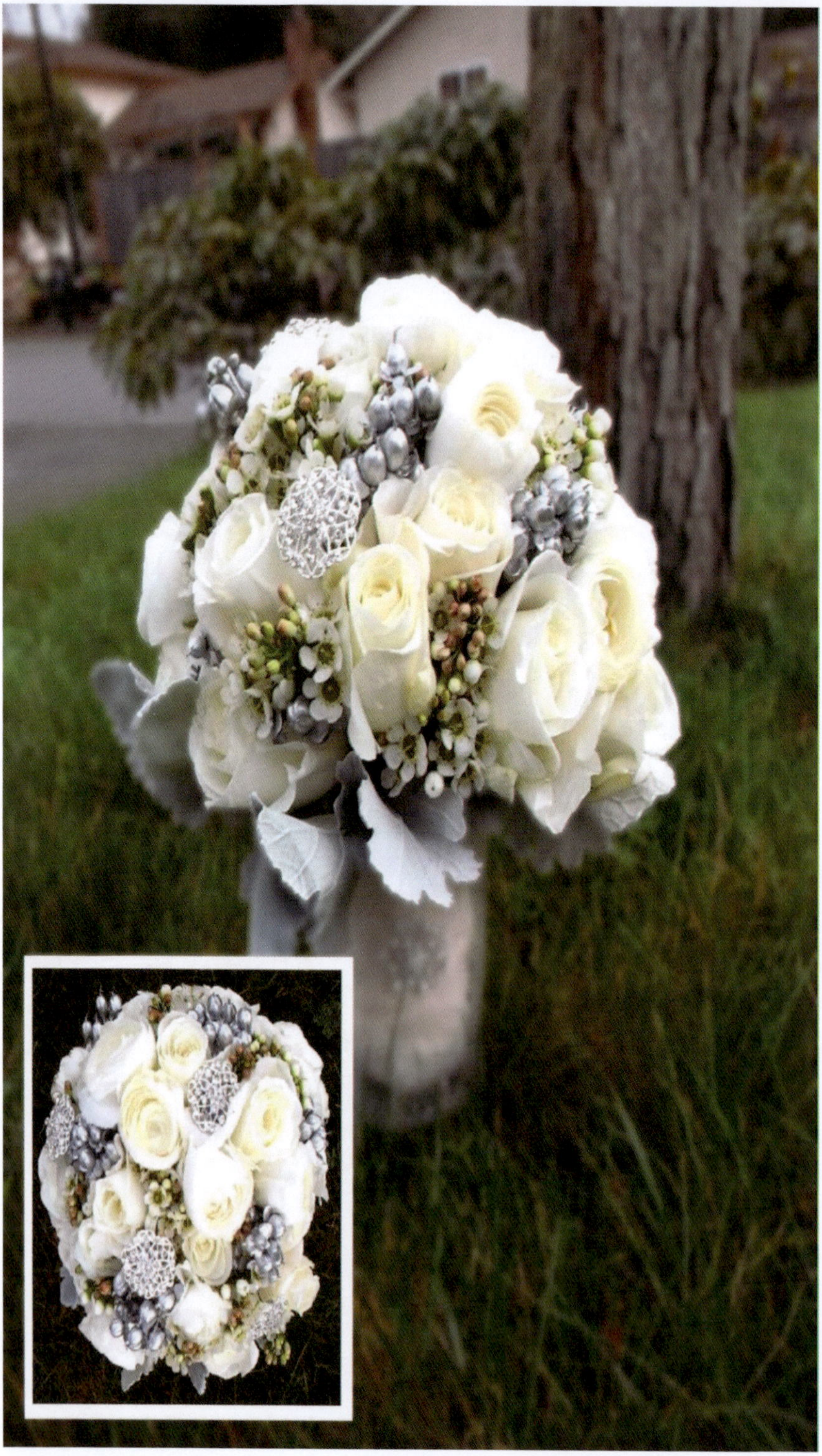

Victorian Ambiance Bouquet

This bouquet spell bounds you with stylish charms.

MATERIALS:

8-12 ivory roses, 8-12 ivory ranunculus, 4-6 silver Colortool spray-painted hypericum berries, 6-8 white wax flowers, 4-6 dusty miller, ivory satin ribbon, pearl brooch, corsage pins, and pruning shears.

INSTRUCTIONS:

1. Prep your flowers by reading the "Condition Your Flowers" section of this book.
2. Gather a couple of wax flowers with one hand like you are holding a bouquet. With your other hand, insert roses one at a time in different spots. Make sure to arrange outwards and downwards into a round, ball pattern. Try not to have flowers stick too far out. Reserve the ranunculus and hypericum berries for later.
3. When you have a basic shape, secure it by wrapping floral tape around it with your free hand.
4. Continue inserting more flowers, but adjust some flowers so new ones fit. Insert the ranunculus and hypericum berries in spots you like. Frame the outside of the bouquet with dusty miller. Secure the final look with floral tape.
5. SAFETY ALERT: Before using the pruning shears to cut the stems to the desired length, pay attention to where your fingers are. Cut away from your fingers and nowhere close to them.
6. Wrap the white satin ribbon around the stem and secure the end of the ribbon by inserting 2-3 pins downward. Pin the brooch on the front.

See "Care Instructions" section for details on proper care.

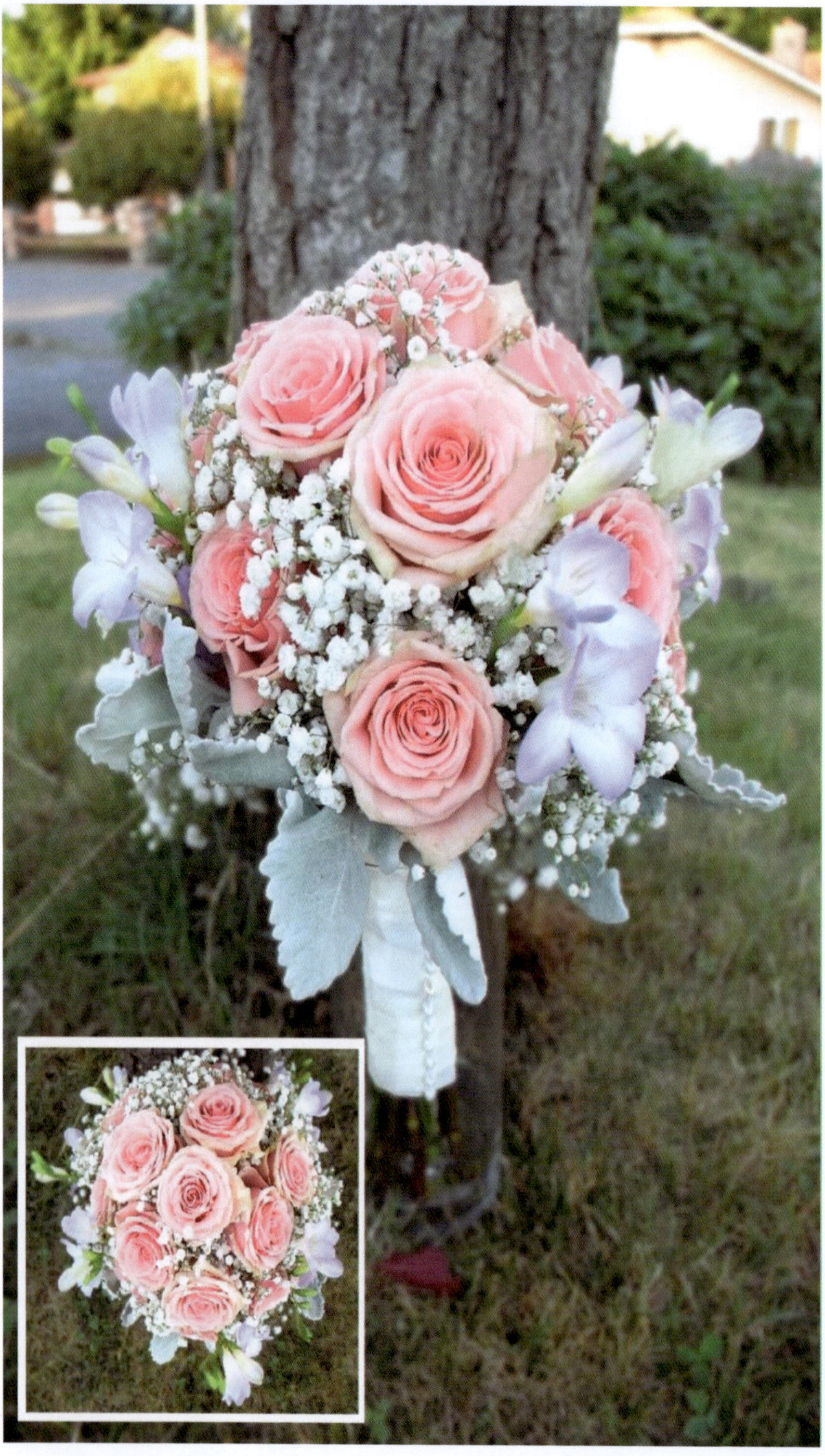

Blush Pink Bouquet

This bouquet is a show-stopper and is very classy.

MATERIALS:

12-20 bloomed pink roses, 4-6 lavender freesias, 6-8 white overtime flowers, 4-6 dusty miller, ivory satin ribbon, corsage pins, and pruning shears.

INSTRUCTIONS:

1. Prep your flowers by reading the "Condition Your Flowers" section of this book.
2. Gather a couple of overtime flowers with one hand like you are holding a bouquet. With your other hand, insert roses one at a time in different spots. Make sure to arrange outwards and downwards into a round, ball pattern. Try not to have flowers stick too far out. Reserve the freesias for later.
3. When you have a basic shape, secure it by wrapping it with floral tape with your free hand.
4. Continue inserting more flowers, but adjust some flowers so new ones fit. Add the freesias in spots you like by inserting the stem into the bouquet. Frame the outside of the bouquet with dusty miller. Secure the final look with floral tape.
5. SAFETY ALERT: Before using the pruning shears to cut the stems to the desired length, pay attention to where your fingers are. Cut away from your fingers and nowhere close to them.
6. Wrap the ivory satin ribbon around the stem and secure the end of the ribbon by inserting 2-3 pins downward.

See "Care Instructions" section for details on proper care.

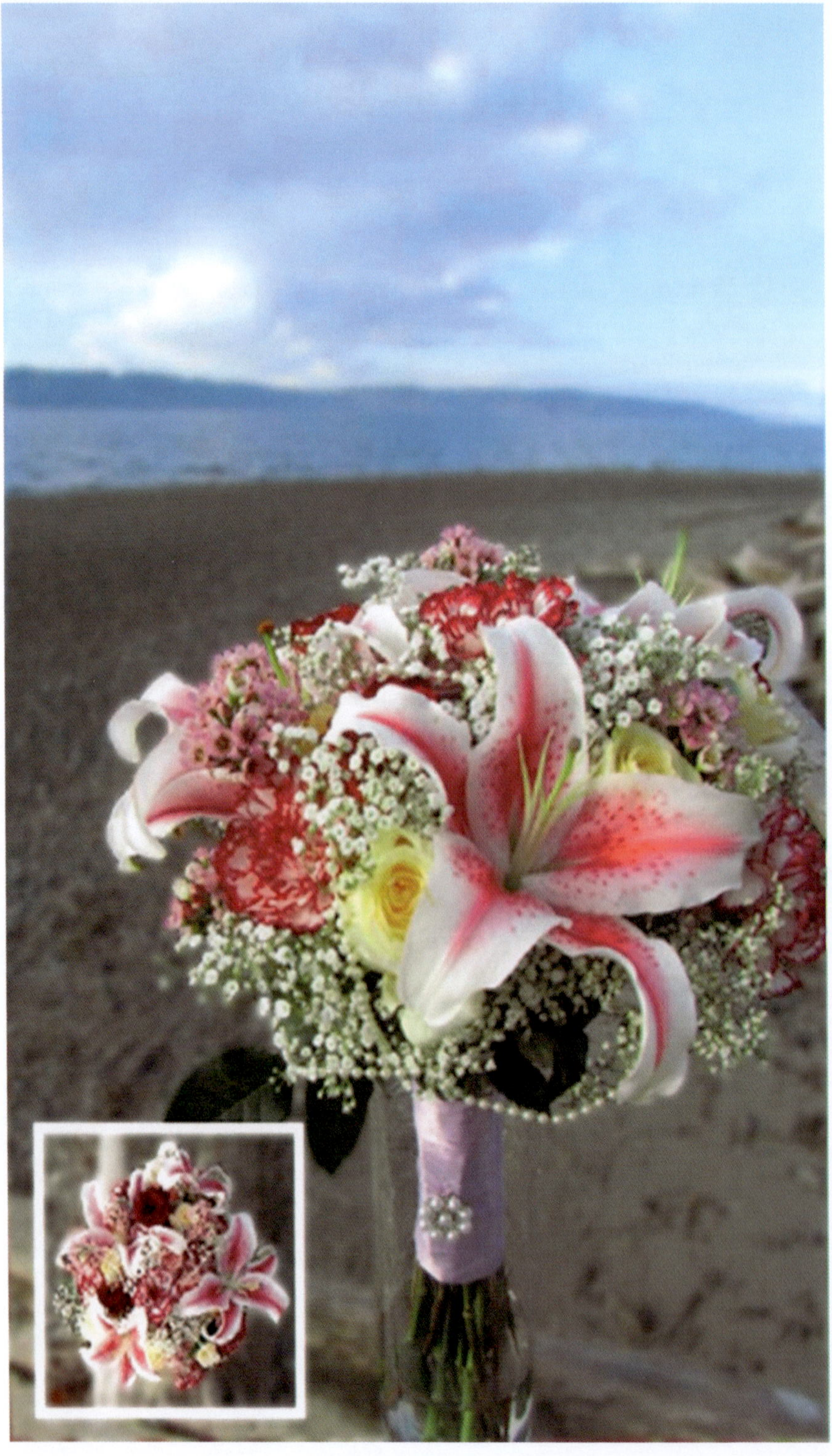

Beach Romance Bouquet

This bouquet is beaming with youthful glamour.

MATERIALS:

4-6 yellow roses, 3-4 fully bloomed pink oriental lilies, 6-8 white overtime flowers, 6-8 red and white blended carnations, lavender satin ribbon, pearl strand, pearl brooch, corsage pins, and pruning shears.

INSTRUCTIONS:

1. Prep your flowers by reading the "Condition Your Flowers" section of this book.
2. Gather a couple of overtime flowers with one hand like you are holding a bouquet. With your other hand, insert other flowers one at a time in different spots. Make sure to arrange outwards and downwards into a round, ball pattern. Try not to have flowers stick too far out. Reserve the lilies for later.
3. When you have a basic shape, secure it by wrapping it with floral tape with your free hand.
4. Continue inserting more flowers, but adjust some flowers so new ones fit. Add the lilies in spots you like by inserting the stem into the bouquet. Secure the final look with floral tape.
5. SAFETY ALERT: Before using the pruning shears to cut the stems to the desired length, pay attention to where your fingers are. Cut away from your fingers and nowhere close to them.
6. Wrap the lavender satin ribbon around the stem and secure the end of the ribbon by inserting 2-3 pins downward. Pin the brooch on the front and lace the pearl strands around the bouquet.

See "Care Instructions" section for details on proper care.

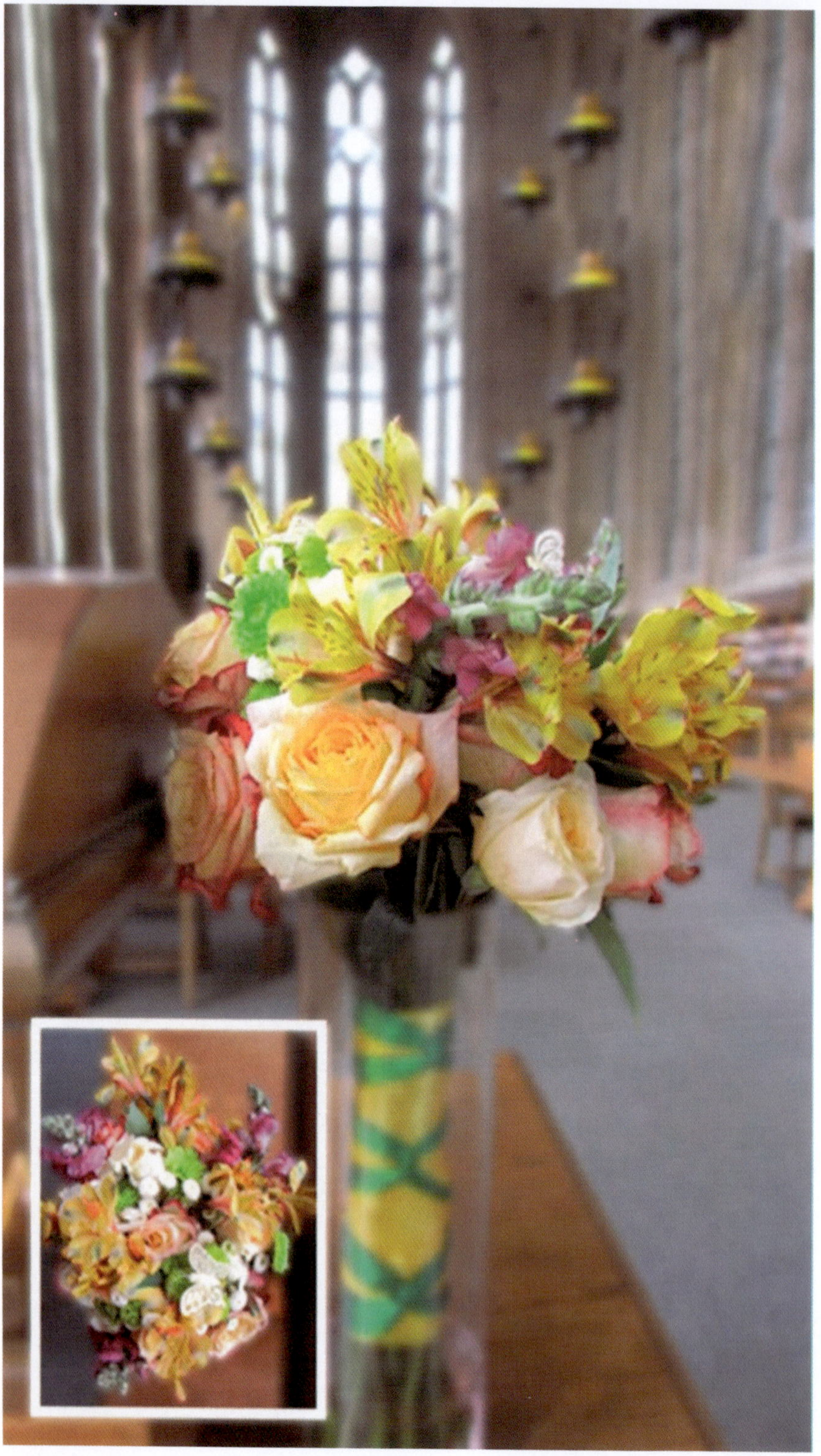

Scholarly Musings Bouquet

This bouquet is inspired by medieval architecture.

MATERIALS:

6-8 yellow roses, 4-6 yellow alstromeri, 2-4 purple alstromeri, 4-6 purple stock, 6-8 pink and ivory blended roses, 4-6 purple snap dragons, 4-6 green mini mums, yellow satin ribbon, thin green satin ribbon, corsage pins, and pruning shears.

INSTRUCTIONS:

1. Prep your flowers by reading the "Condition Your Flowers" section of this book.
2. Gather a couple of flowers with one hand like you are holding a bouquet. With your other hand, insert other flowers one at a time in different spots. Make sure to arrange outwards and downwards into a round, ball pattern. Try not to have flowers stick too far out. When you have a basic shape, secure it by wrapping floral tape around it with your free hand.
3. Continue inserting more flowers, but adjust some flowers so new ones fit. Secure the final look with floral tape.
4. SAFETY ALERT: Before using the pruning shears to cut the stems to the desired length, pay attention to where your fingers are. Cut away from your fingers and nowhere close to them.
5. Wrap the yellow satin ribbon around the stem and secure the end of the ribbon by inserting 2-3 pins downward. Wrap the thin green ribbon around in a criss-cross design and pin the intersections as you go, then pin the end of the ribbon back or tuck it inside the bouquet.

See "Care Instructions" section for details on proper care.

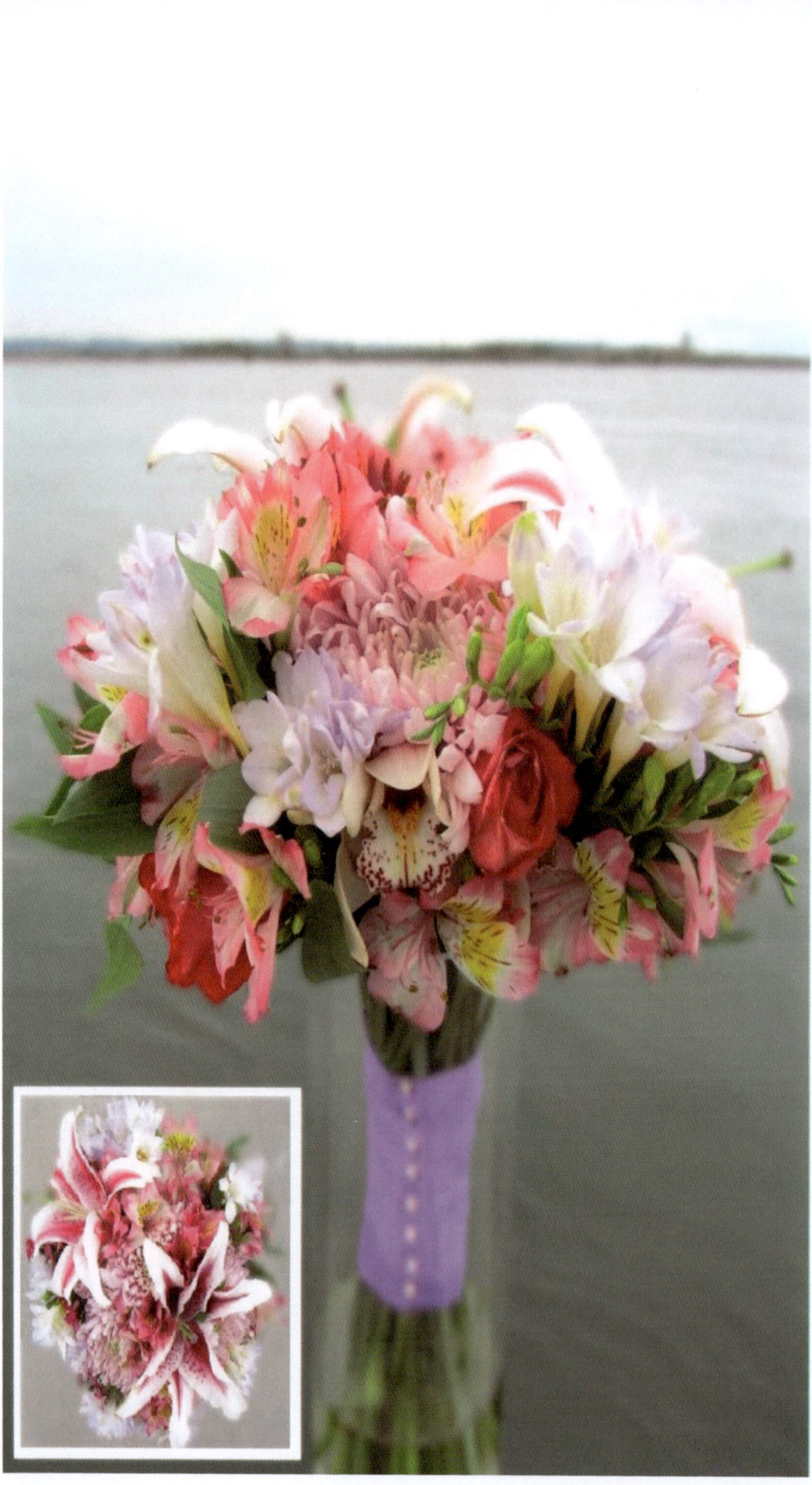

Friendship First Bouquet

This bouquet is inspired by flowers you can safely give to somebody you fancy and it is non-comital while you get to know each other.

MATERIALS:

4-6 pink alstromeri, 2-4 white alstromeri, 4-6 pink poms, 6-8 lavender freesias, 6-8 red roses, 2-3 fully opened pink oriental lilies, lavender satin ribbon, corsage pins, and pruning shears.

INSTRUCTIONS:

1. Prep your flowers by reading the "Condition Your Flowers" section of this book.
2. Gather a couple of flowers like you are holding a bouquet. With your other hand, insert other flowers one at a time in different spots. Make sure to arrange outwards and downwards into a round, ball pattern. Try not to have flowers stick too far out. When you have a basic shape, secure it by wrapping floral tape around it with your free hand.
3. Continue inserting more flowers, but adjust some flowers so new ones fit. Secure the final look with floral tape.
4. SAFETY ALERT: Before using the pruning shears to cut the stems to the desired length, pay attention to where your fingers are. Cut away from your fingers and nowhere close to them.
5. Wrap the satin ribbon around the stem and secure the end of the ribbon by inserting 2-3 pins downward, then add pins up along the sides.

See "Care Instructions" section for details on proper care.

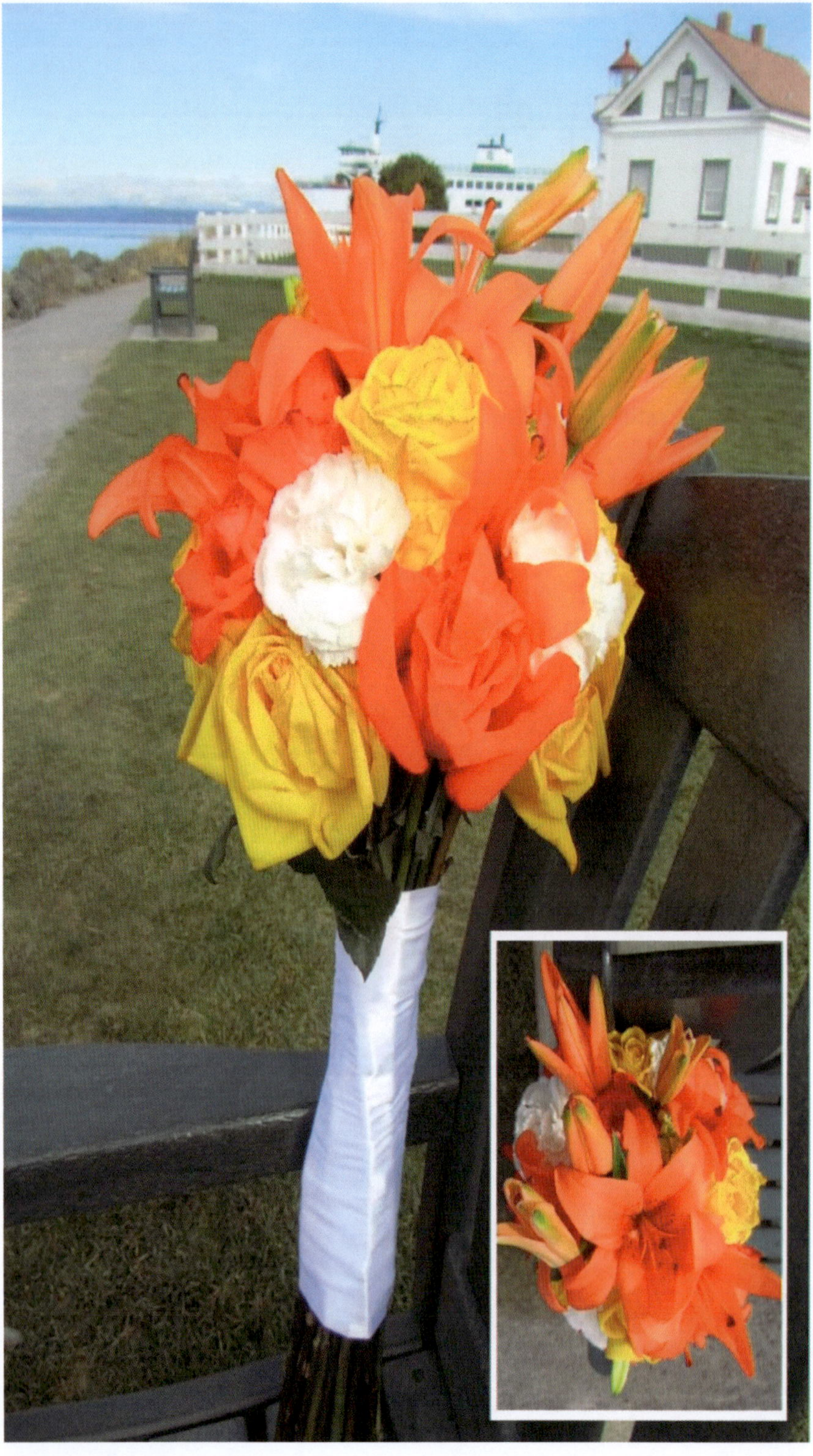

Year Round Flowers Bouquet

You will not have to worry about seasons with this bouquet full of flowers that are available at stores year round.

MATERIALS:

6-8 orange roses, 6-8 yellow roses, 6-8 white carnations, 2-3 opened orange Asiatic lilies, white satin ribbon, corsage pins, and pruning shears.

INSTRUCTIONS:

1. Prep your flowers by reading the "Condition Your Flowers" section of this book.
2. Gather a couple flowers with one hand like you are holding a bouquet. With your other hand, insert other flowers one at a time in different spots. Make sure to arrange outwards and downwards into a round, ball pattern. When you have a basic shape, secure it by wrapping floral tape around it with your free hand. Reserve the lilies.
3. Continue inserting more flowers, then insert the lilies where desired. Secure the final look with floral tape.
4. SAFETY ALERT: Before using the pruning shears to cut the stems to the desired length, pay attention to where your fingers are. Cut away from your fingers and nowhere close to them.
5. Wrap the satin ribbon around the stem and secure the end of the ribbon by inserting 2-3 pins downward and pins along the backside.

See "Care Instructions" section for details on proper care.

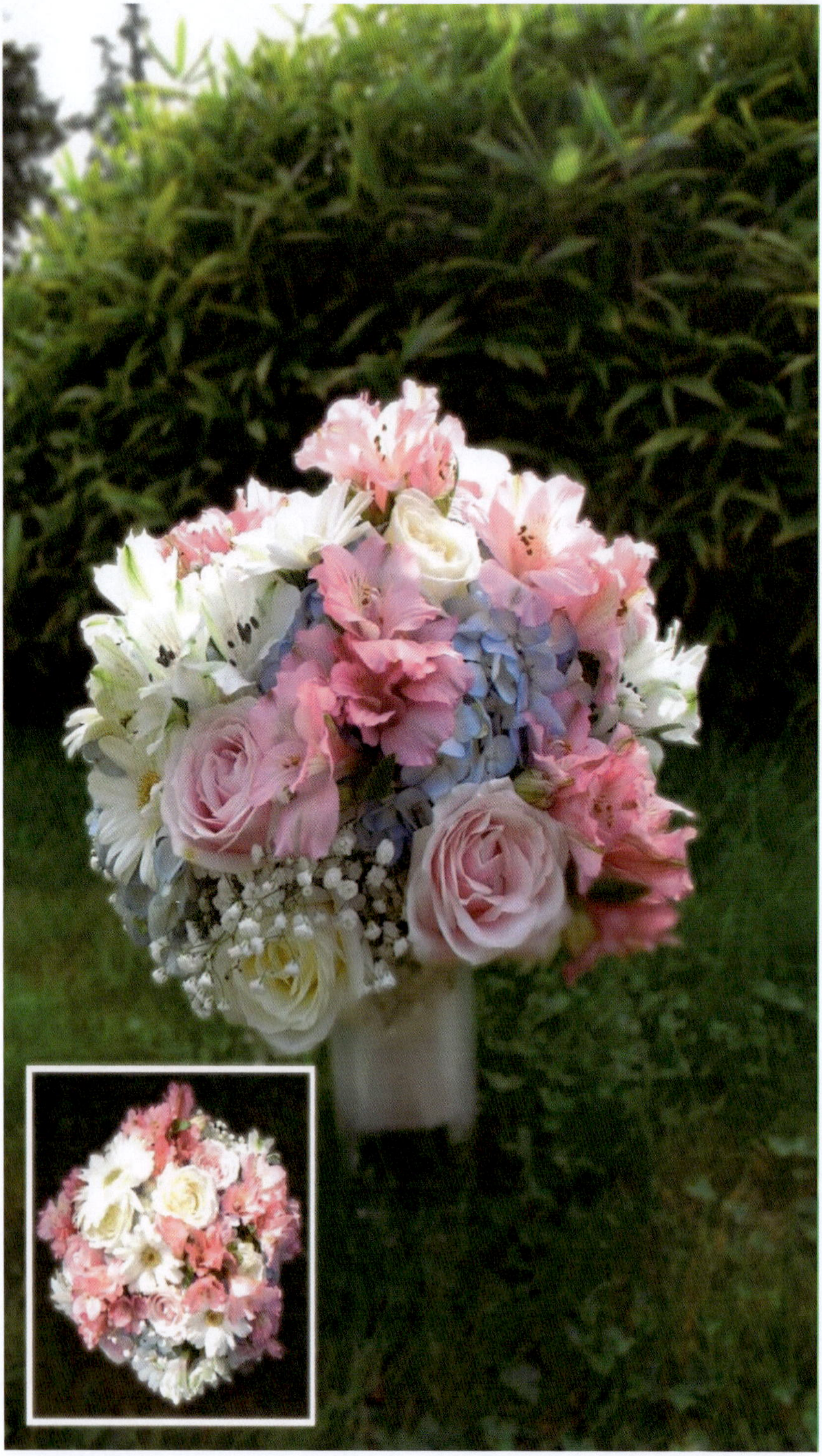

Early Spring Bouquet

Theses flowers are available in early spring, just in time for your wedding.

MATERIALS:

6-8 pink roses, 6-8 white roses, 4-6 overtime, 2-3 blue hydrangeas, 3-6 pink alstromeri, 3-6 white alstromeri, 4-6 white gerbera daisies, white satin ribbon, corsage pins, and pruning shears.

INSTRUCTIONS:

1. Prep your flowers by reading the "Condition Your Flowers" section of this book.
2. Gather a couple of overtime flowers with one hand like you are holding a bouquet. With your other hand, insert other flowers one at a time in different spots. Make sure to arrange outwards and downwards into a round, ball pattern. When you have a basic shape, secure it by wrapping floral tape around it with your free hand.
3. Continue inserting more flowers. Secure the final look with floral tape.
4. SAFETY ALERT: Before using the pruning shears to cut the stems to the desired length, pay attention to where your fingers are. Cut away from your fingers and nowhere close to them.
5. Wrap the satin ribbon around the stem and secure the end of the ribbon by inserting 2-3 pins downward and pins along the back.

See "Care Instructions" section for details on proper care.

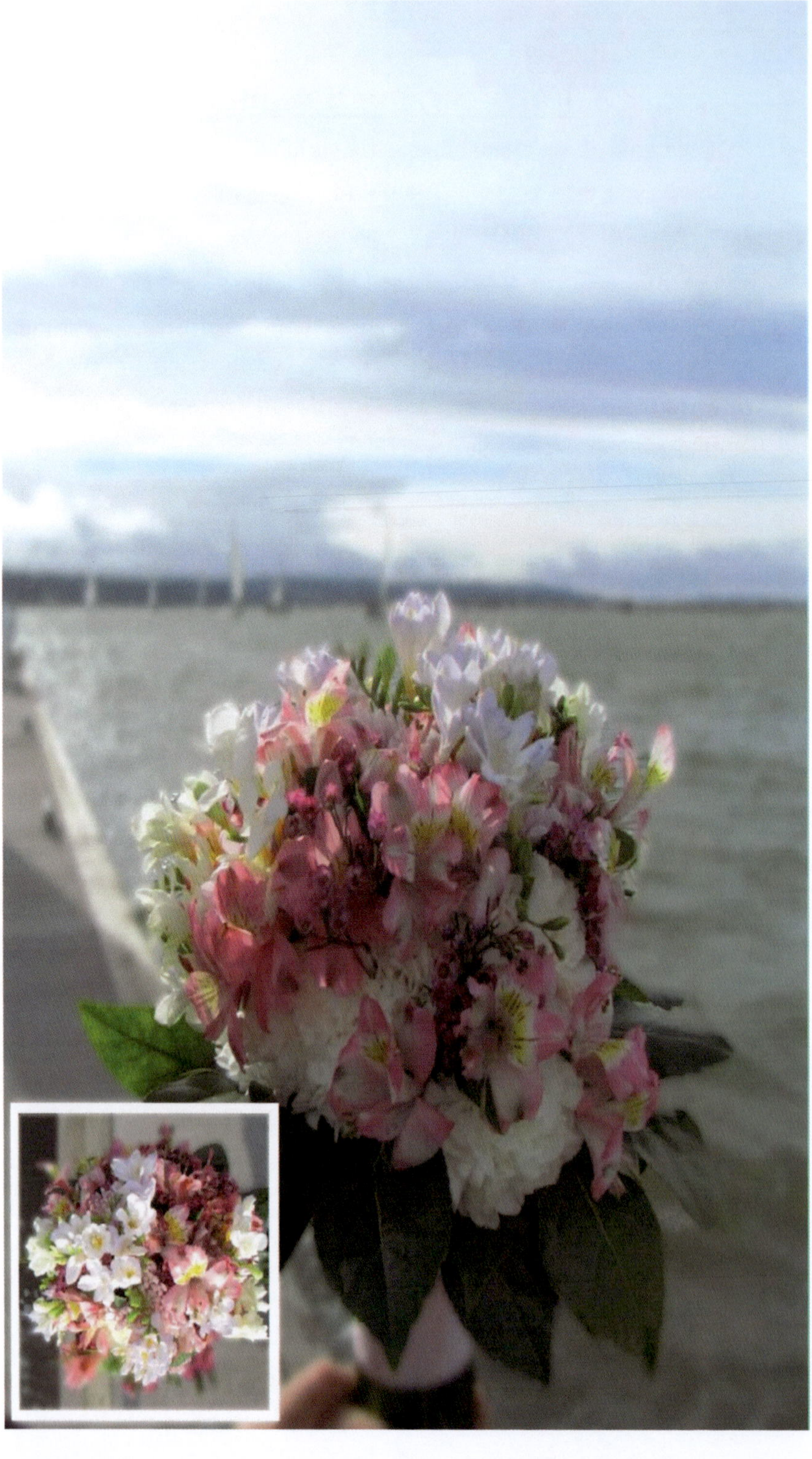

Spring Breeze Bouquet

You will be swept away by the movement the leaves give in framing this delightful bouquet.

MATERIALS:

4-6 white hydrangeas, 8-12 pink alstromeri, 6-8 lavender freesias, 6-8 ivory freesias, 6-8 salal regular green leaves, white satin ribbon, corsage pins, and pruning shears.

INSTRUCTIONS:

1. Prep your flowers by reading the "Condition Your Flowers" section of this book.
2. Gather a couple hydrangeas with one hand like you are holding a bouquet. With your other hand, insert other flowers one at a time in different spots and pull the stems down from the bottom to the desired height. Make sure to arrange outwards and downwards into a round, ball pattern. When you have a basic shape, secure it by wrapping floral tape around it with your free hand.
3. Continue inserting more flowers. When the final look is satisfactory, then gather the leaves around the bouquet. Secure the final look with floral tape.
4. SAFETY ALERT: Before using the pruning shears to cut the stems to the desired length, pay attention to where your fingers are. Cut away from your fingers and nowhere close to them.
5. Wrap the satin ribbon around the stem and secure the end of the ribbon by inserting 2-3 pins downward and pins along the back.

See "Care Instructions" section for details on proper care.

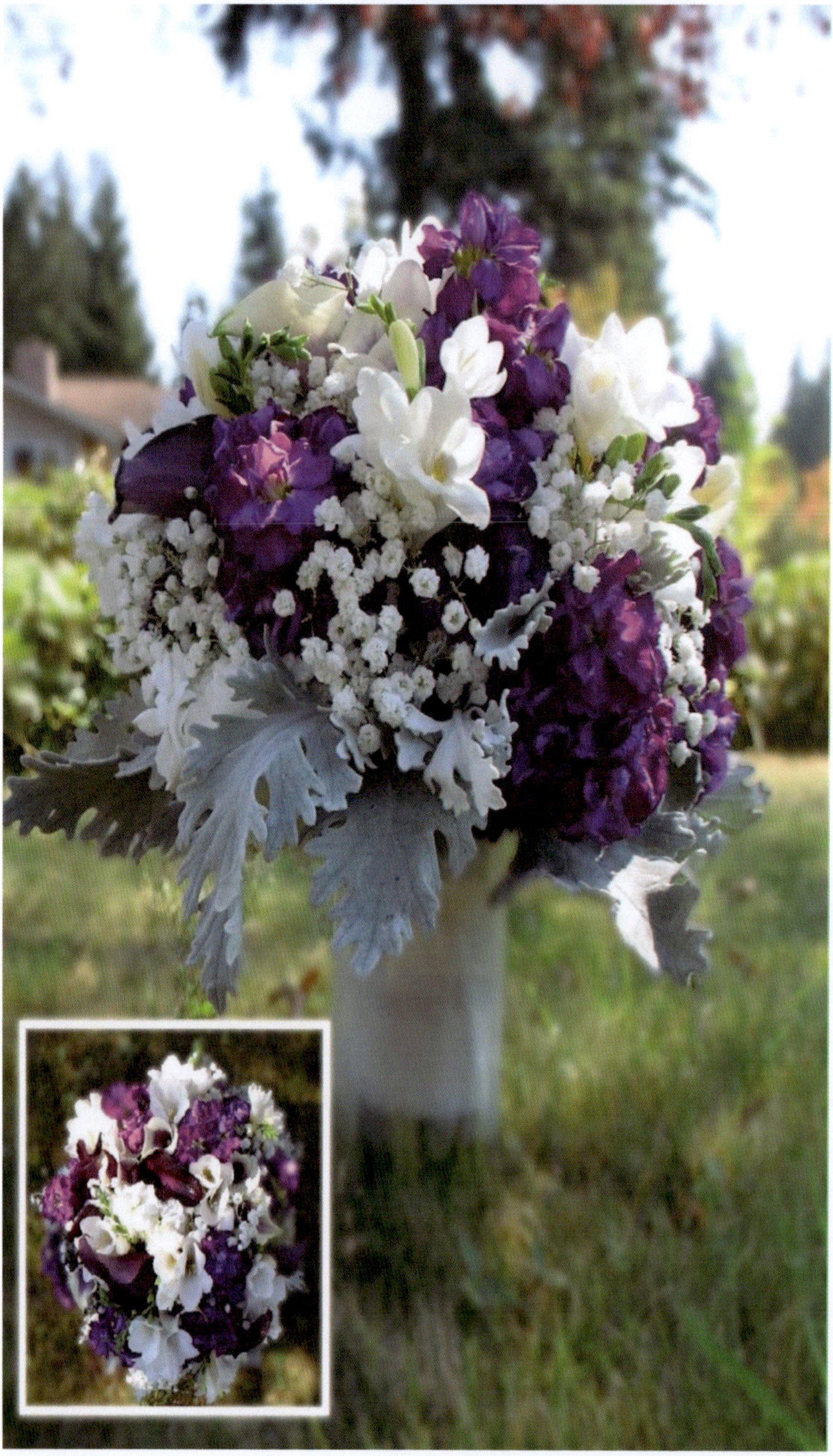

Plum Accents Bouquet

You cannot miss the plum purple flowers
that accent this glorious white bouquet.

MATERIALS:

6-8 overtime, 8-12 dark plum purple stock, 8-12 white freesias, 6-8 white calla lilies, 6-8 plum calla lilies, 6-8 dusty miller, white satin ribbon, corsage pins, and pruning shears.

INSTRUCTIONS:

1. Prep your flowers by reading the "Condition Your Flowers" section of this book.
1. Gather a couple of overtime flowers with one hand like you are holding a bouquet. With your other hand, insert other flowers one at a time in different spots. Reserve the freesias for later. Make sure to arrange outwards and downwards into a round, ball pattern. When you have a basic shape, secure it by wrapping floral tape around it with your free hand.
2. Continue inserting more flowers. Insert the freesias in different spots where desired. When the final look is achieved, gather the dusty miller around the bouquet and secure the final look with floral tape.
3. SAFETY ALERT: Before using the pruning shears to cut the stems to the desired length, pay attention to where your fingers are. Cut away from your fingers and nowhere close to them.
4. Wrap the satin ribbon around the stem and secure the end of the ribbon by inserting 2-3 pins downward and pins along the back.

See "Care Instructions" section for details on proper care.

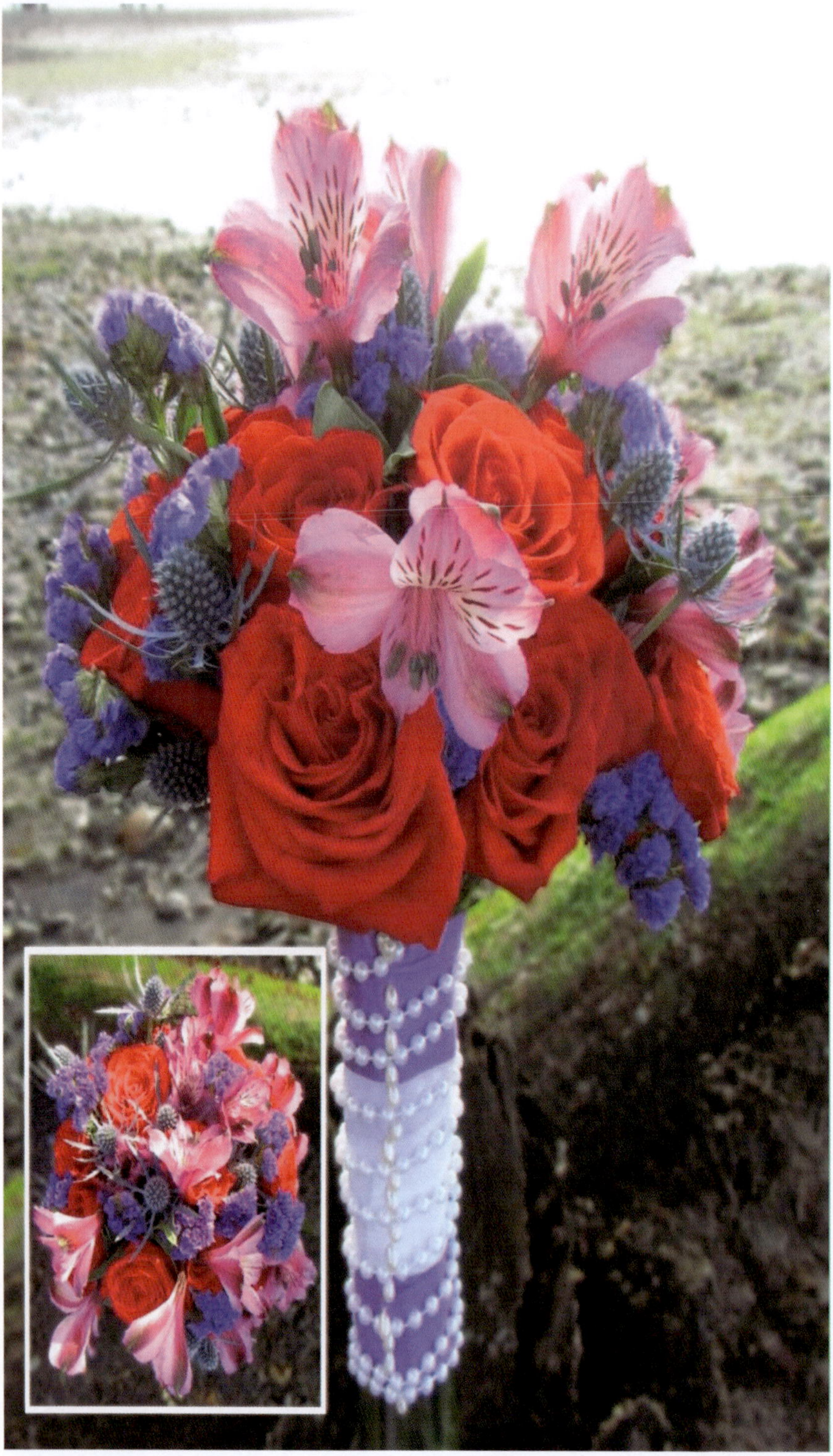

Uniquely Yours Bouquet

The one-of-a-kind flare comes out
in this unique design.

MATERIALS:

6-8 purple alstromeri, 8-10 thistle, 12-16 red roses, 6-8 purple static, white satin ribbon, purple satin ribbon, pearl strand, corsage pins, and pruning shears.

INSTRUCTIONS:

1. Prep your flowers by reading the "Condition Your Flowers" section of this book.
2. Gather a couple of roses and static with one hand like you are holding a bouquet. With your other hand, insert other flowers one at a time in different spots. Reserve the thistle and alstromeri for later. Make sure to arrange outwards and downwards into a round, ball pattern. Wrap the basic shape with floral tape using your free hand.
1. Continue inserting more flowers. Insert the thistle and alstromeri where desired making sure they sit above the rose layer. Secure the final look with floral tape.
2. SAFETY ALERT: Before using the pruning shears to cut the stems to the desired length, pay attention to where your fingers are. Cut away from your fingers and nowhere close to them.
3. Wrap the purple ribbon around the stem and secure the end of the ribbon by inserting 2-3 pins downward. Wrap the white ribbon over it and secure with a pin. Then wrap the pearl strand around it and secure with pins. Insert pints along the back in a row.

See "Care Instructions" section for details on proper care.

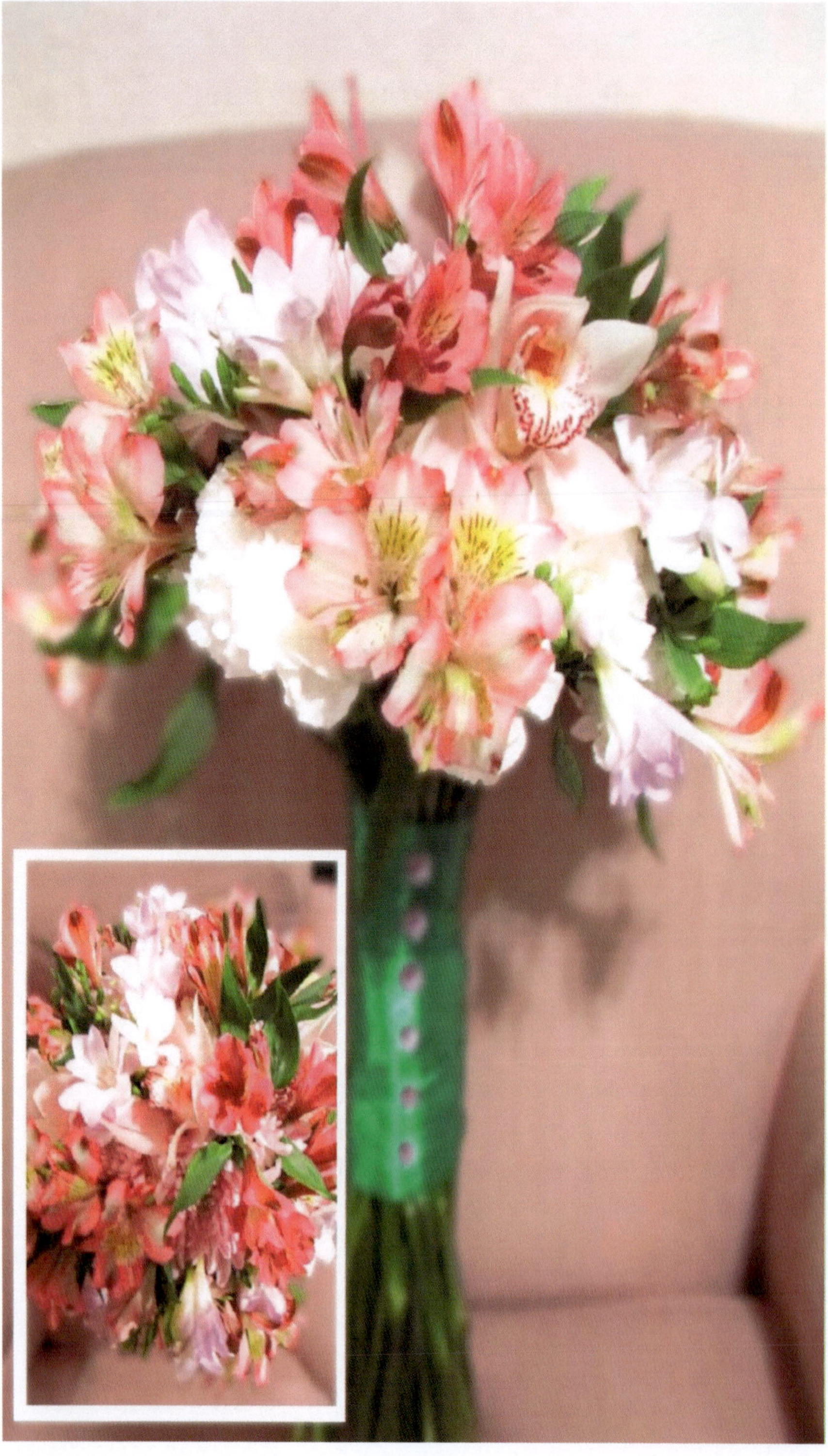

Dainty Delights Bouquet

This bouquet features many dainty flowers that tickle your senses.

MATERIALS:

8-12 white carnations, 6-8 pink alstromeri, 6-8 purple alstromeri, 6-8 white alstromeri, 6-8 lavender freesias, 3-6 cymbidium orchids held in floral tubes, green satin ribbon, corsage pins, hot glue gun, rhinestones, and pruning shears.

INSTRUCTIONS:

1. Prep your flowers by reading the "Condition Your Flowers" section of this book.
2. Gather a couple of carnations with one hand like you are holding a bouquet. The carnations are the base layer. With your other hand, insert other flowers one at a time in different spots. Make sure to arrange outwards and downwards into a round, ball pattern. When you have a basic shape, secure it by wrapping floral tape around it with your free hand.
3. Continue inserting more flowers, and then secure the final look with floral tape.
4. SAFETY ALERT: Before using the pruning shears to cut the stems to the desired length, pay attention to where your fingers are. Cut away from your fingers and nowhere close to them.
5. Wrap the satin ribbon around the stem and secure the end of the ribbon by inserting 2-3 pins downward and pins along the back. Hot glue rhinestones along the ribbon.

See "Care Instructions" section for details on proper care.

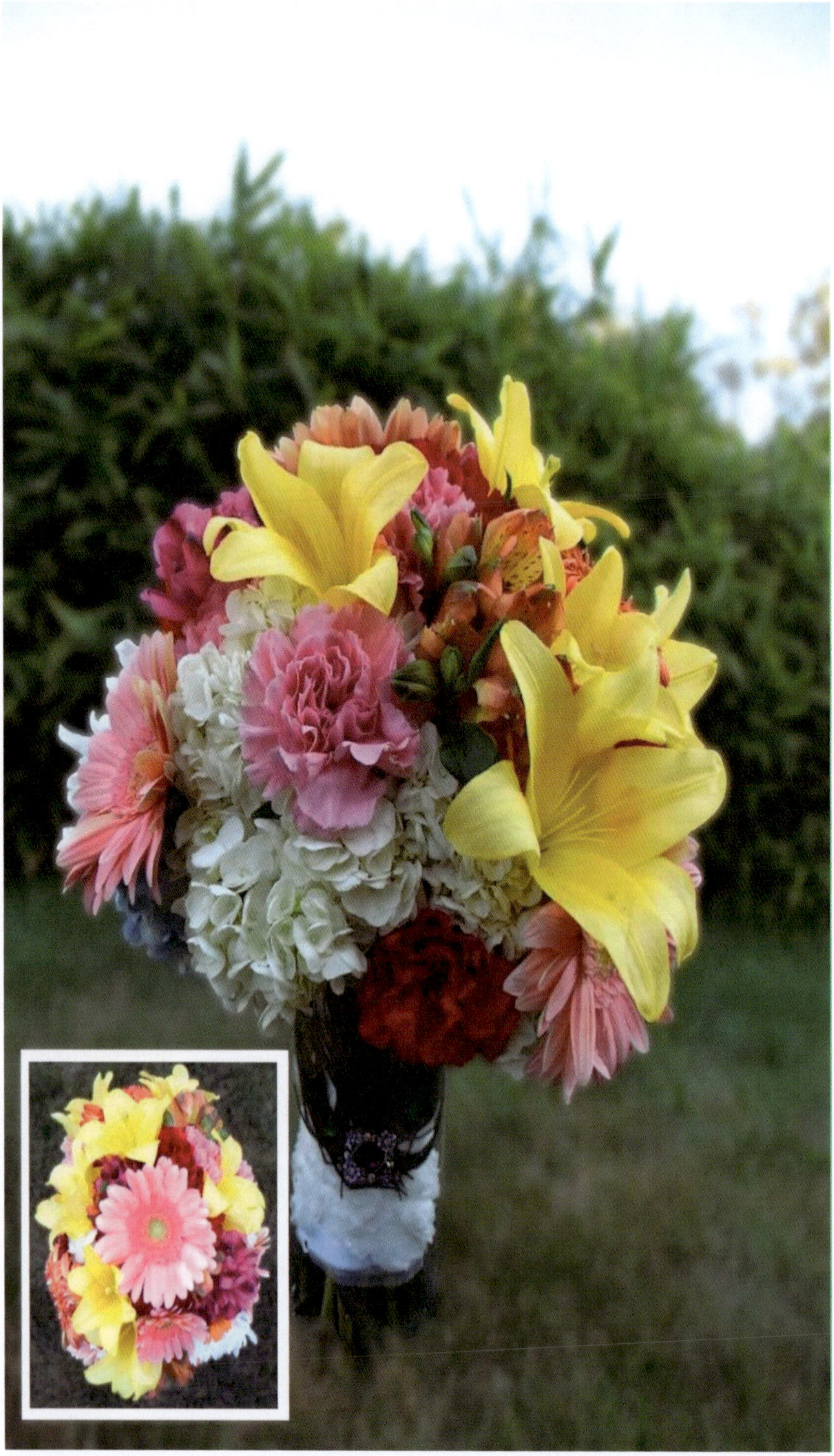

Happy Flowers Bouquet

All seasonal flowers of a great summer wedding are in full bloom with this bouquet.

MATERIALS:

4-6 white hydrangea, 6-8 yellow Asiatic lilies, 6-8 pink gerbera daisies, 6-8 orange alstromeri, 8-10 pink carnations, 6-8 red carnations, white lace ribbon, brooch, corsage pins, and pruning shears.

INSTRUCTIONS:

1. Prep your flowers by reading the "Condition Your Flowers" section of this book.
2. Gather a couple hydrangeas with one hand like you are holding a bouquet. With your other hand, insert other flowers one at a time in different spots. Reserve the lilies and gerbera daisies for later. Make sure to arrange outwards and downwards into a round, ball pattern. Wrap the basic shape with floral tape using your free hand.
3. Continue inserting more flowers. Insert the lilies and gerbera daisies where desired. Secure the final look with floral tape.
4. SAFETY ALERT: Before using the pruning shears to cut the stems to the desired length, pay attention to where your fingers are. Cut away from your fingers and nowhere close to them.
5. Wrap the lace ribbon around the stem and secure the end of the ribbon by inserting 2-3 pins downward and pins along the back. Pin brooch to the front.

See "Care Instructions" section for details on proper care.

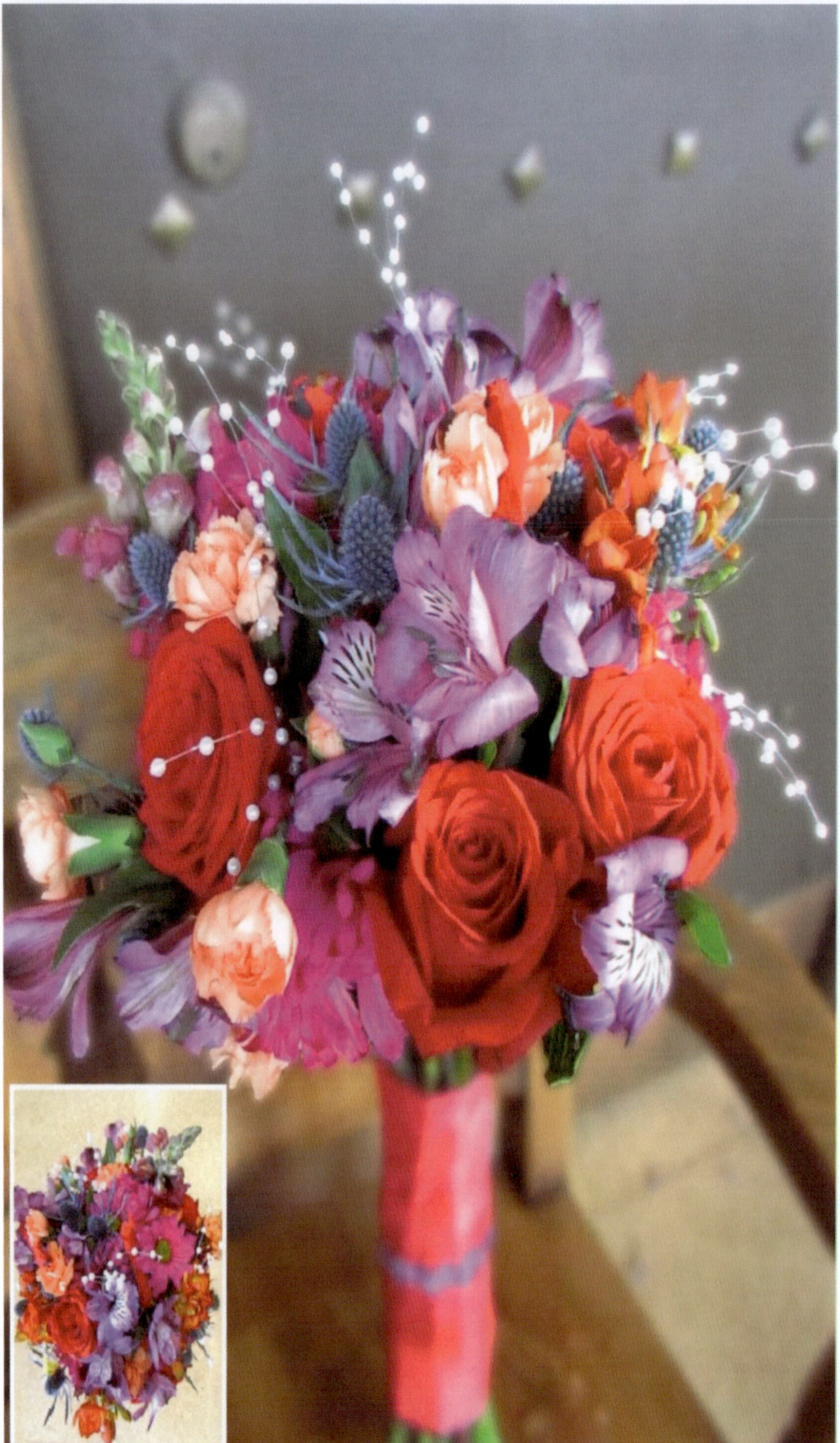

Baroque Remembrance Bouquet

The appeal of the Baroque period in art history is remembered in this colorful mix brought up-to-date.

MATERIALS:

8-12 red roses, 8-12 orange mini carnations, 8-12 purple alstromeri, 6-8 purple stock flowers, 8-12 thistle, 6-8 hot pink carnations, pearl shoots, hot pink satin ribbon, thin purple ribbon, corsage pins, and pruning shears.

INSTRUCTIONS:

1. Prep your flowers by reading the "Condition Your Flowers" section of this book.
2. Gather a couple of flowers with one hand like you are holding a bouquet. With your other hand, insert other flowers one at a time in different spots. Make sure to arrange outwards and downwards into a round, ball pattern. Wrap the basic shape with floral tape using your free hand.
3. Continue inserting more flowers. Secure the final look with floral tape.
4. SAFETY ALERT: Before using the pruning shears to cut the stems to the desired length, pay attention to where your fingers are. Cut away from your fingers and nowhere close to them.
5. Wrap the satin ribbon around the stem and secure the end of the ribbon by inserting 2-3 pins downward and pins along the back. Tie the thin purple ribbon on the mid-section of the stem.

See "Care Instructions" section for details on proper care.

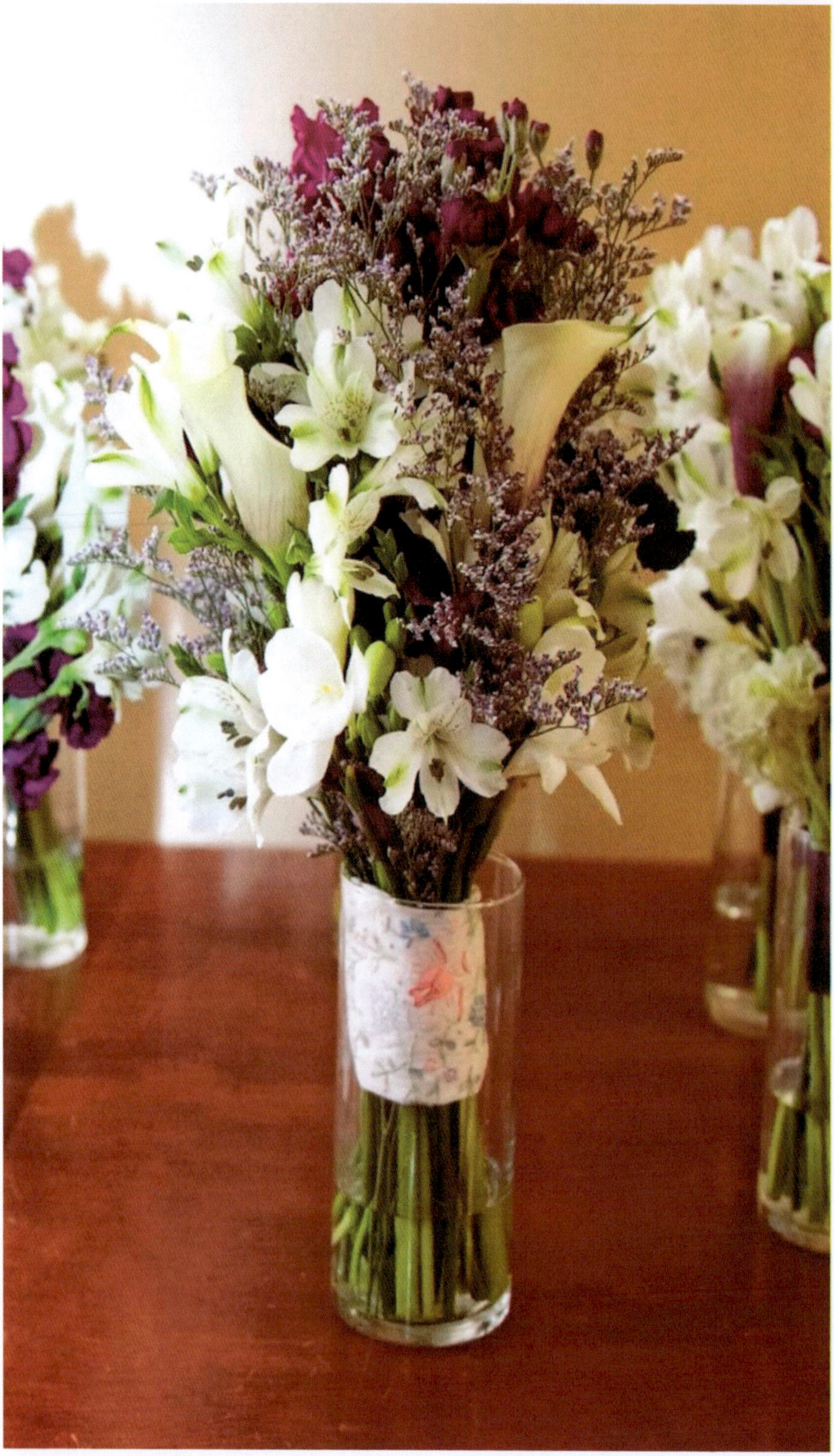

Extraordinarily Unique Bouquet

This varied shape is a unique design that will set you apart from the pack and will hold sentimental value for the bride.

MATERIALS:

8-12 heather, 12-18 dark plum mini carnations, 6-8 dark purple stock flowers, 8-12 white calla lily, 8-12 white freesia, sentimental handkerchief, corsage pins, and pruning shears.

INSTRUCTIONS:

1. Prep your flowers by reading the "Condition Your Flowers" section of this book.
2. Gather a couple of heather flowers with one hand like you are holding a bouquet. With your other hand, insert other flowers one at a time in different spots making sure to vary the heights. Reserve the freesias for later. Make sure to arrange outwards and downwards into a round, long ball pattern. Wrap the basic shape with floral tape using your free hand.
3. Continue inserting more flowers. Insert the freesias where desired, making sure the flowers are seen. Secure the final look with floral tape.
4. SAFETY ALERT: Before using the pruning shears to cut the stems to the desired length, pay attention to where your fingers are. Cut away from your fingers and nowhere close to them.
5. Wrap the handkerchief around the stem and secure the end of the handkerchief by inserting 2-3 pins downward and pins along the back.

See "Care Instructions" section for details on proper care.

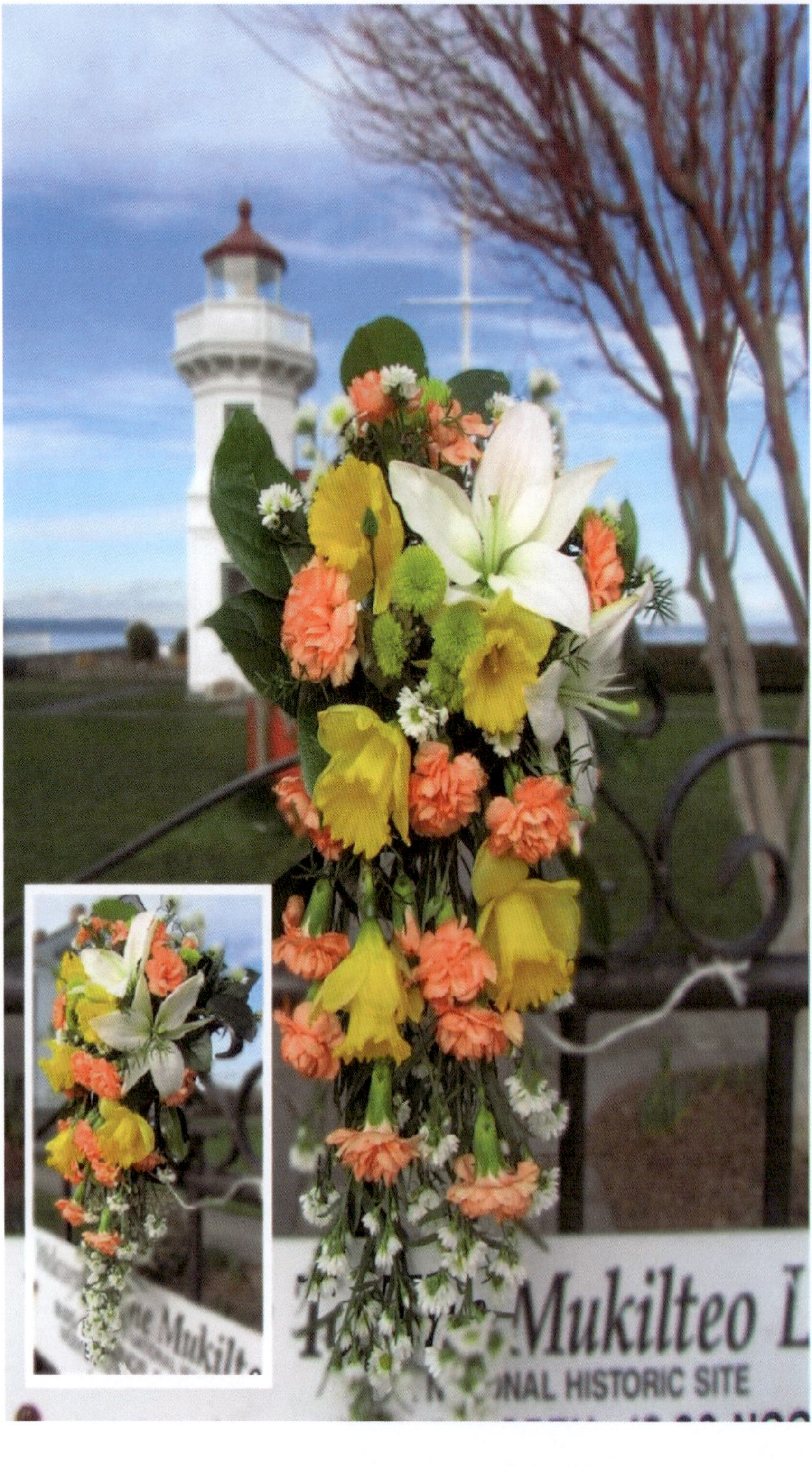
Mukilteo
HISTORIC SITE

Daffodils in Spring Bouquet

Cascading bouquets have made a comeback with royal weddings and showcase daffodils well.

MATERIALS:

4-6 monte casinos, 2-3 white Asiatic lilies, 8-12 orange carnations, 8-12 daffodils, 6-8 green mini mums, 4-6 salal green leaves, cascading bouquet holder, floral lock-stem adhesive spray, hot-glue gun, thick velvet ribbon, short vase, plastic saran wrap, and pruning shears.

INSTRUCTIONS:

1. Prep your flowers by reading the "Condition Your Flowers" section of this book.
2. Hot-glue the thick velvet ribbon to cover the handle of the bouquet holder. Then cover the ribbon with plastic saran wrap to prevent it from getting wet. Now, dunk the foam part of the holder into water for a couple of minutes until soaked. Let it drain for a few minutes and set the holder handle on a short vase with the foam sitting up facing you.
3. Begin inserting the long monte casino flowers at the end of the bouquet to display the longest section. From here you will insert other flowers at the ends and slowly shorten the lengths as you move closer to the center of the bouquet, filling out the sides to create thickness. Insert flowers to fill in the center and insert leaves around the sides to frame the top. Use smaller flowers to fill in open areas. When the desired look is completed, then seal the flowers to the foam by inserting the adhesive spray on the foam between the flowers.

See "Care Instructions" section for details on proper care.

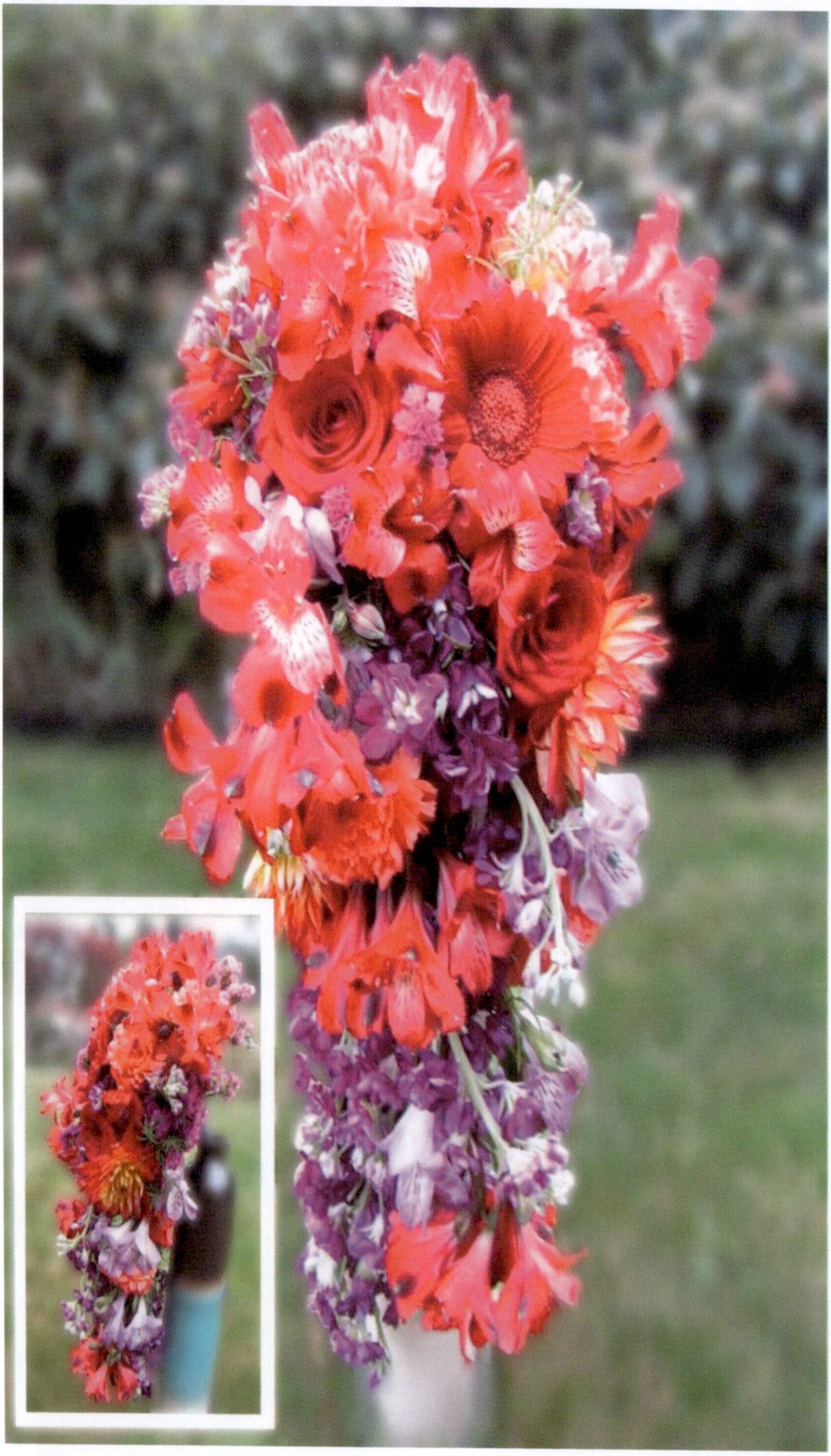

Rouge Bisou Bouquet

You will feel like the red flowers in this cascading bouquet kissed you with love.

MATERIALS:

4-6 purple wax flowers, 4-6 red alstromeri, 4-6 purple stock, 8-12 red roses, 6-8 red dahlia, 6-8 red gerbera daisy, 4-6 purple alstromeri, cascading bouquet holder, floral lock-stem adhesive spray, hot-glue gun, thick velvet ribbon, short vase, plastic saran wrap, and pruning shears.

INSTRUCTIONS:

1. Prep your flowers by reading the "Condition Your Flowers" section of this book.
2. Hot-glue the thick velvet ribbon to cover the handle of the bouquet holder, then cover the ribbon with saran wrap to prevent it from getting wet. Now, dunk the foam part of the holder into water for a couple of minutes until soaked. Let it drain for a few minutes and set the holder handle on a short vase with the foam sitting up facing you.
3. Begin inserting the long stock flowers and alstromeri at the end of the bouquet to display the longest section, then insert more to create thickness and complete an under-layer. Insert long roses over the under-layer and slowly shorten the lengths as you move closer to the center of the bouquet, filling out the sides to create thickness. Begin inserting other flowers. Fill in the gaps with wax flowers. When the desired look is completed, insert the adhesive spray on the foam between the flowers to seal.

See "Care Instructions" section for details on proper care.

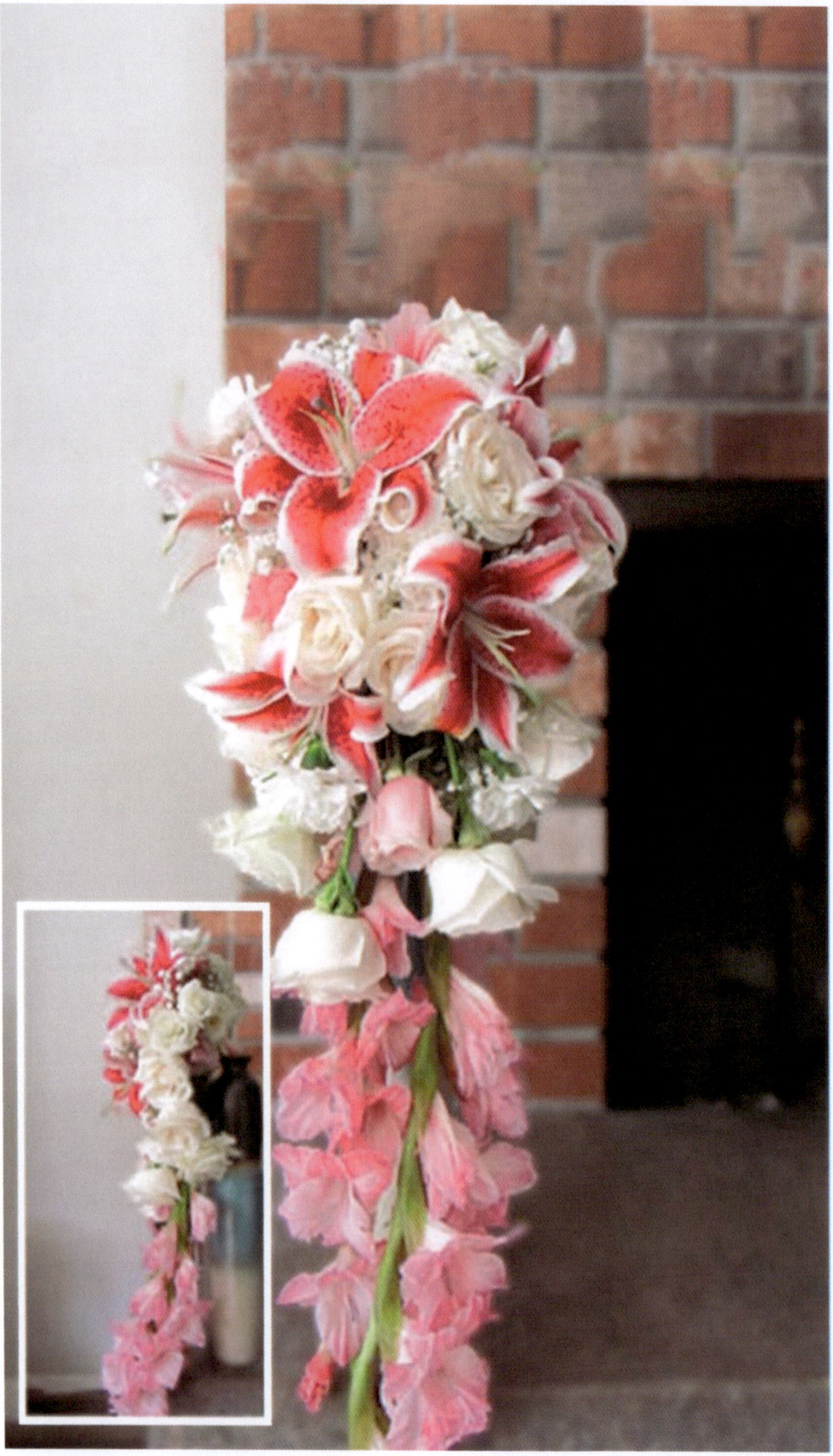

Blush Pink Bouquet

The elegance in this two-tone combination makes us blush with this charming cascading bouquet.

MATERIALS:

4-6 overtime, 2-3 pink gladioli, 2-3 pink oriental lilies, 8-12 white roses, 8-12 pink roses, 6-8 white carnations, cascading bouquet holder, floral lock-stem adhesive spray, hot-glue gun, thick velvet ribbon, short vase, plastic saran wrap, and pruning shears.

INSTRUCTIONS:

1. Prep your flowers by reading the "Condition Your Flowers" section of this book.
2. Hot-glue the thick velvet ribbon to cover the handle of the bouquet holder, then cover the ribbon with saran wrap to prevent it from getting wet. Now, dunk the foam part of the holder into water for a couple of minutes until soaked. Let it drain for a few minutes and set the holder handle on a short vase with the foam sitting up facing you.
3. Begin inserting the long gladioli at the end of the bouquet to display the longest section, then insert more gladioli to create thickness and completes an under-layer. Insert long roses over the gladioli and slowly shorten the lengths as you move closer to the center of the bouquet, filling out the sides to create thickness. Begin inserting other flowers. Fill in gaps with overtime flowers. When the desired look is completed, insert the adhesive spray on the foam between the flowers to seal.

See "Care Instructions" section for details on proper care.

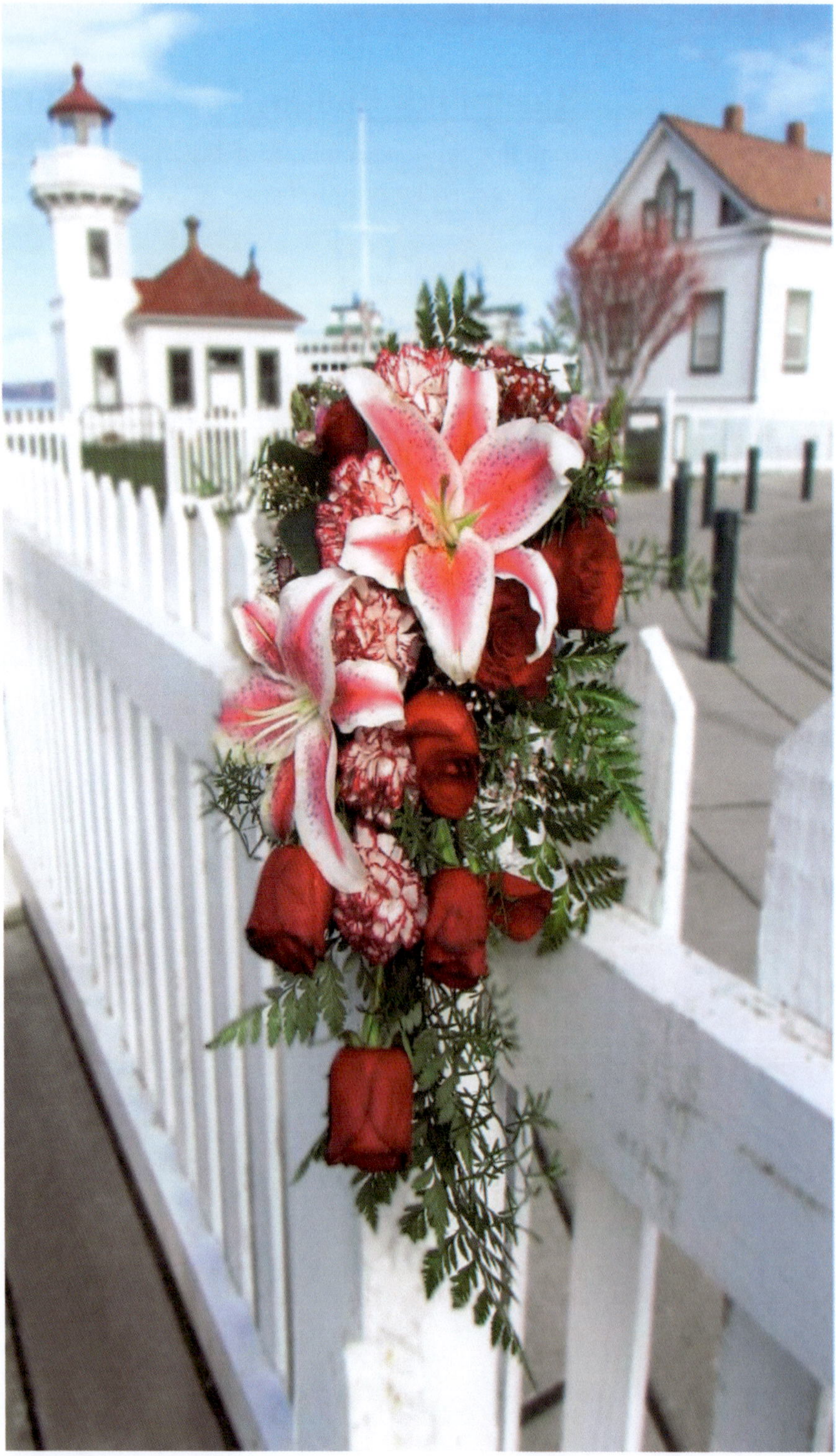

Amour Duree de Vie Bouquet

Translated as, "love of a lifetime". This cascading bouquet brings back turn-of-the century romance.

MATERIALS:

4-6 ferns, 2-3 white-pink oriental lilies, 8-12 red and white blended carnations, 8-12 red roses, 6-8 sprengeri fern, 3-5 fern leaves, leaf shine, cascading bouquet holder, floral lock-stem adhesive spray, hot-glue gun, thick velvet ribbon, short vase, plastic saran wrap, and pruning shears.

INSTRUCTIONS:

1. Prep your flowers by reading the "Condition Your Flowers" section of this book.
2. Hot-glue the thick velvet ribbon to cover the handle of the bouquet holder, then cover the ribbon with saran wrap to prevent it from getting wet. Dunk the foam part of the holder into water for a couple of minutes until soaked and let drain for a few minutes and set the holder handle on a short vase with the foam sitting up facing you.
3. Begin inserting the long fern leaves at the end of the bouquet to create the long section. Insert sprengeri ferns leaves in the center to complete a green under-layer and spray with leaf shine. Insert flowers in the ends and slowly shorten the lengths as you move closer to the center of the bouquet, filling out the sides to create thickness. When the desired look is completed, insert the adhesive spray on the foam between the flowers to seal.

See "Care Instructions" section for details on proper care.

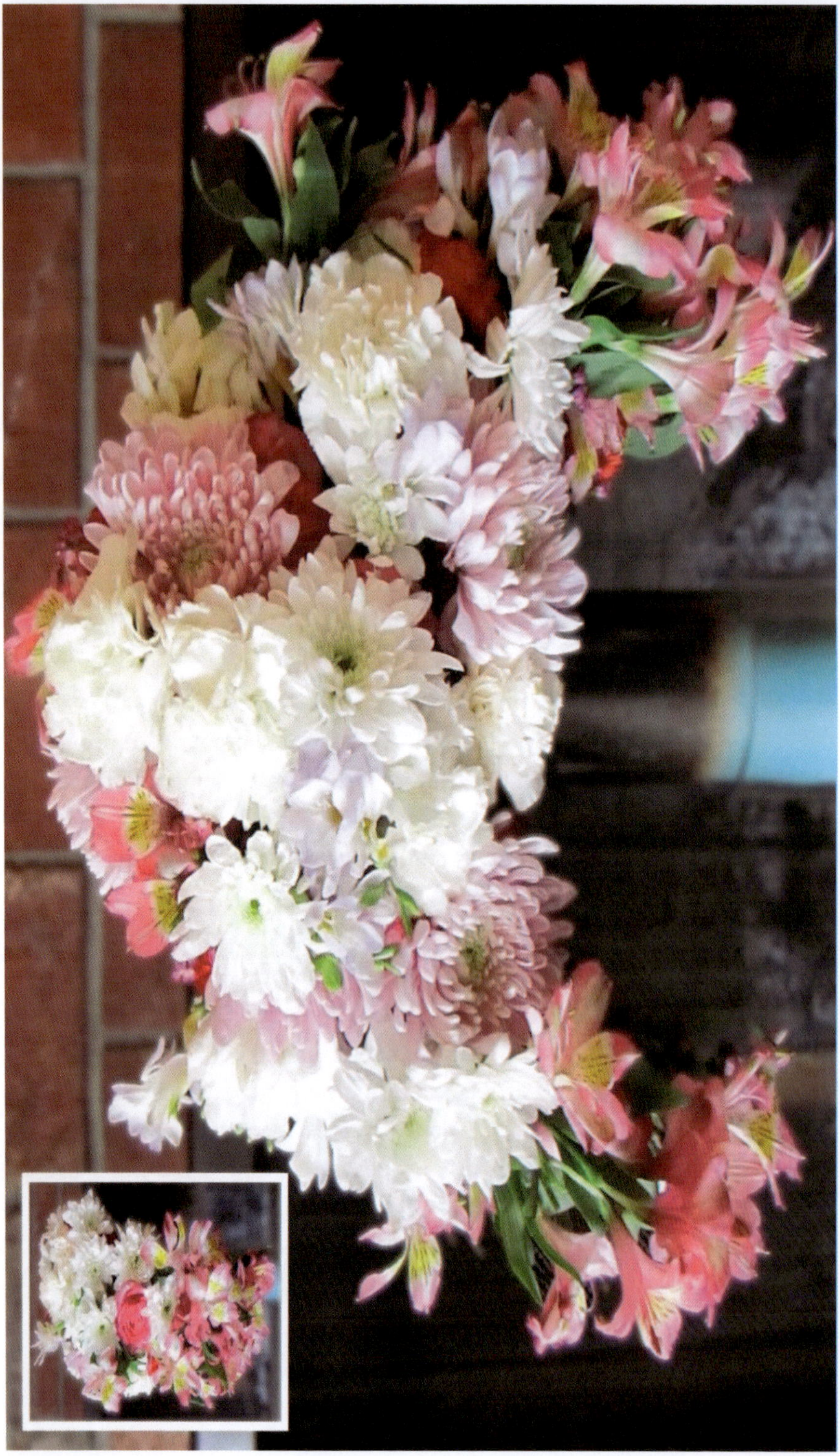

Nous Nous Marions Bouquet

"Nous nous marions" is French for "We're getting married!" This crescent bouquet looks like it is the announcement from all sides.

MATERIALS:

4-6 pink alstromeri, 4-6 white alstromeri 6-8 large pink spider mums, 4-6 large white spider mums, 6-8 mini white mums, cascading bouquet holder, floral lock-stem adhesive spray, hot-glue gun, thick velvet ribbon, short vase, plastic saran wrap, and pruning shears.

INSTRUCTIONS:

1. Prep your flowers by reading the "Condition Your Flowers" section of this book.
2. Hot-glue the thick velvet ribbon to cover the handle of the bouquet holder, then cover the ribbon with saran wrap to prevent it from getting wet. Now, dunk the foam part of the holder into water for a couple of minutes until soaked. Let it drain for a few minutes and set the holder handle on a short vase with the foam sitting up facing you.
3. Insert the long alstromeri at both ends of the bouquet, then insert more alstromeri to create thickness. Insert other flowers and slowly shorten the lengths as you move closer to the center of the bouquet, filling out the sides to create thickness. When the desired look is completed, insert the adhesive spray on the foam between the flowers to seal.

See "Care Instructions" section for details on proper care.

2
Boutonnieres & Corsages

Alstromeria, Carnation, and Wax Flowers

MATERIALS:

1-2 pink alstromeri, 1-2 white carnation, pink wax flowers, green floral tape, 2 corsage pins, and shears.

INSTRUCTIONS:

1. Gather a carnation, an alstromeri, and wax flowers together with one hand to get the desired look, then wrap the base of the stems together with floral tape using your other hand. Double the recipe for corsages.
2. When a good thickness is achieved, press the end of the tape to the stem to seal it.
3. SAFETY ALERT: Before using the pruning shears to cut the stems to the desired length, pay attention to where your fingers are. Cut away from your fingers and nowhere close to them.

See "Care Instructions" section for details on proper care.

Rose, Carnation, and Wax Flowers

MATERIALS:

1-2 pink roses, 1-2 red mini carnations, 1-2 red wax flowers, bow, green floral tape, 2 corsage pins, and shears

INSTRUCTIONS:

1. Gather flowers together with one hand to get the desired look, then wrap the base of the stems together with floral tape using your other hand. Double the recipe for corsages.
2. When a good thickness is achieved, press the tape to the stem to seal it. Wrap bow with more tape.
3. SAFETY ALERT: Before using the pruning shears to cut the stems to the desired length, pay attention to where your fingers are. Cut away from your fingers and nowhere close to them.

See "Care Instructions" section for details on proper care.

Rose, Mini Carnation, and Ribbon

MATERIALS:

1-2 orange mini carnations, 1-2 red rose, green bow, green floral tape, 2 corsage pins, wrist bracelets, oasis floral adhesive, pearl shoots, and shears

INSTRUCTIONS:

1. Follow boutonniere instructions from previous examples. For the wrist corsage, glue floral adhesive to the base of the bracelet and let dry a little. SAFETY ALERT: While using shears, cut away from your fingers and nowhere close to them.
2. Add bow, pearl shoots, and flowers into the glue where desired and add glue to base to secure.

See "Care Instructions" section for details on proper care.

Rose, Stock, and Ribbon

MATERIALS:

1-2 stock flowers, 1 yellow rose, lace bow, green floral tape, 2 corsage pins, wrist bracelets, oasis floral adhesive, and shears.

INSTRUCTIONS:

1. Follow boutonniere instructions from previous examples. For the wrist corsage, glue floral adhesive to the base of the bracelet and let dry a little. SAFETY ALERT: While using shears, cut away from your fingers and nowhere close to them.
2. Add bow and flowers into the glue where desired and add glue to base to secure.

See "Care Instructions" section for details on proper care.

3
Altar Arrangements

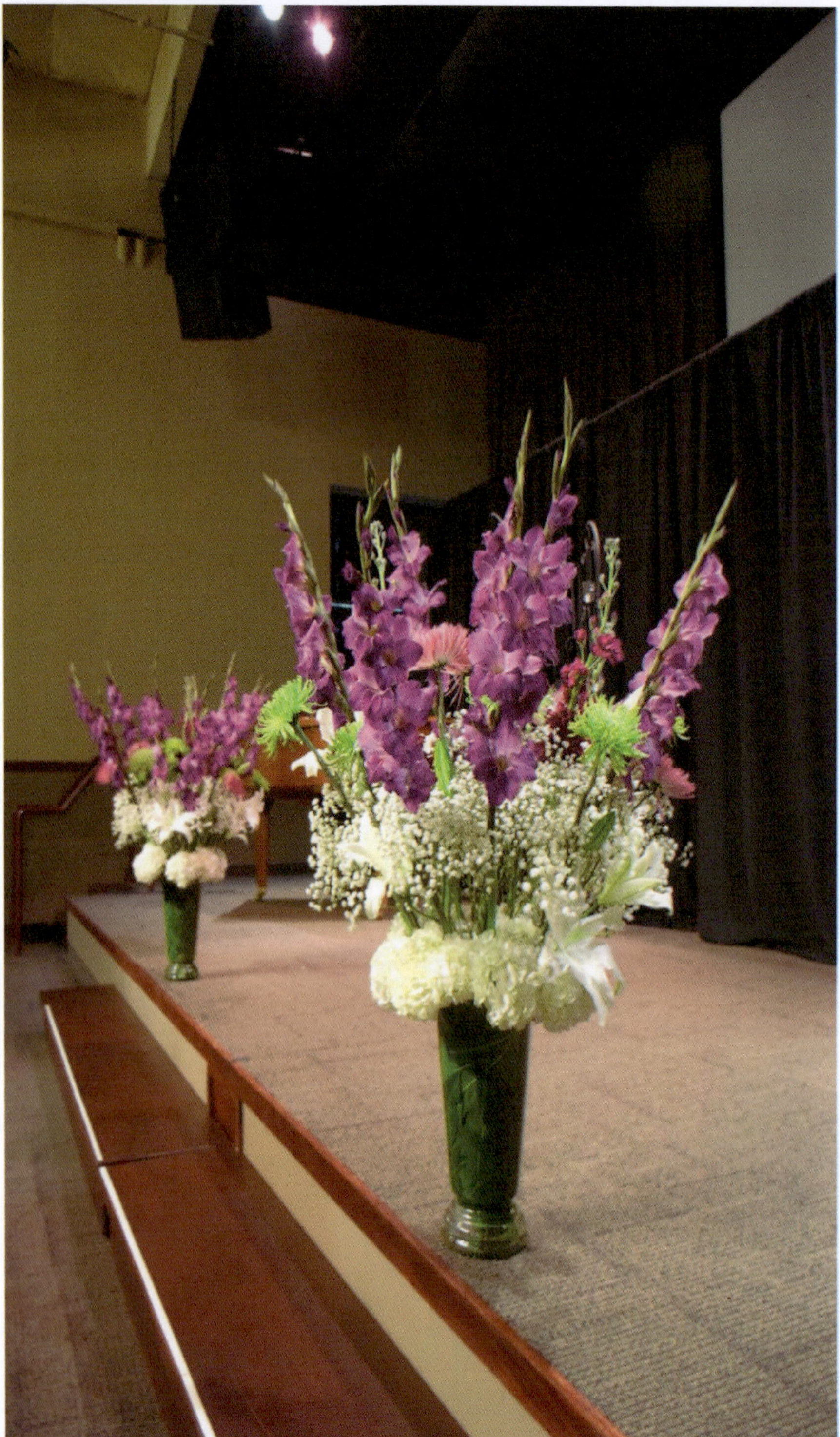

Sprayed Out Altar Vase Arrangement

Tall flowers sprayed out in a vase can be made a couple of days in advance, and enjoyed for another two weeks afterwards.

MATERIALS:

Tall vase(s), 4-6 Japanese fatsias, 8-10 hydrangeas, 8-12 fully opened oriental lilies, 8-12 overtime, 12-16 spider mums, 12-16 gladioli, oasis clear tape.

INSTRUCTIONS:

1. Prep your flowers by reading the "Condition Your Flowers" section of this book.
2. Cover the inside of the vase with fatsia leaves to mask the stems, fill with water and flower food. Create a grid pattern with oasis clear tape on the top of the vase.
3. Insert all the overtime flowers to create the base layer, then insert other flowers where desired. Be sure to space the flowers accordingly and arrange the height evenly as well. When the final look is achieved, insert the hydrangeas on the inside edge of the vase to frame the flowers. Mist the flowers with water and check the water levels often as hydrangeas drink a lot of water quickly.

See "Care Instructions" section for details on proper care.

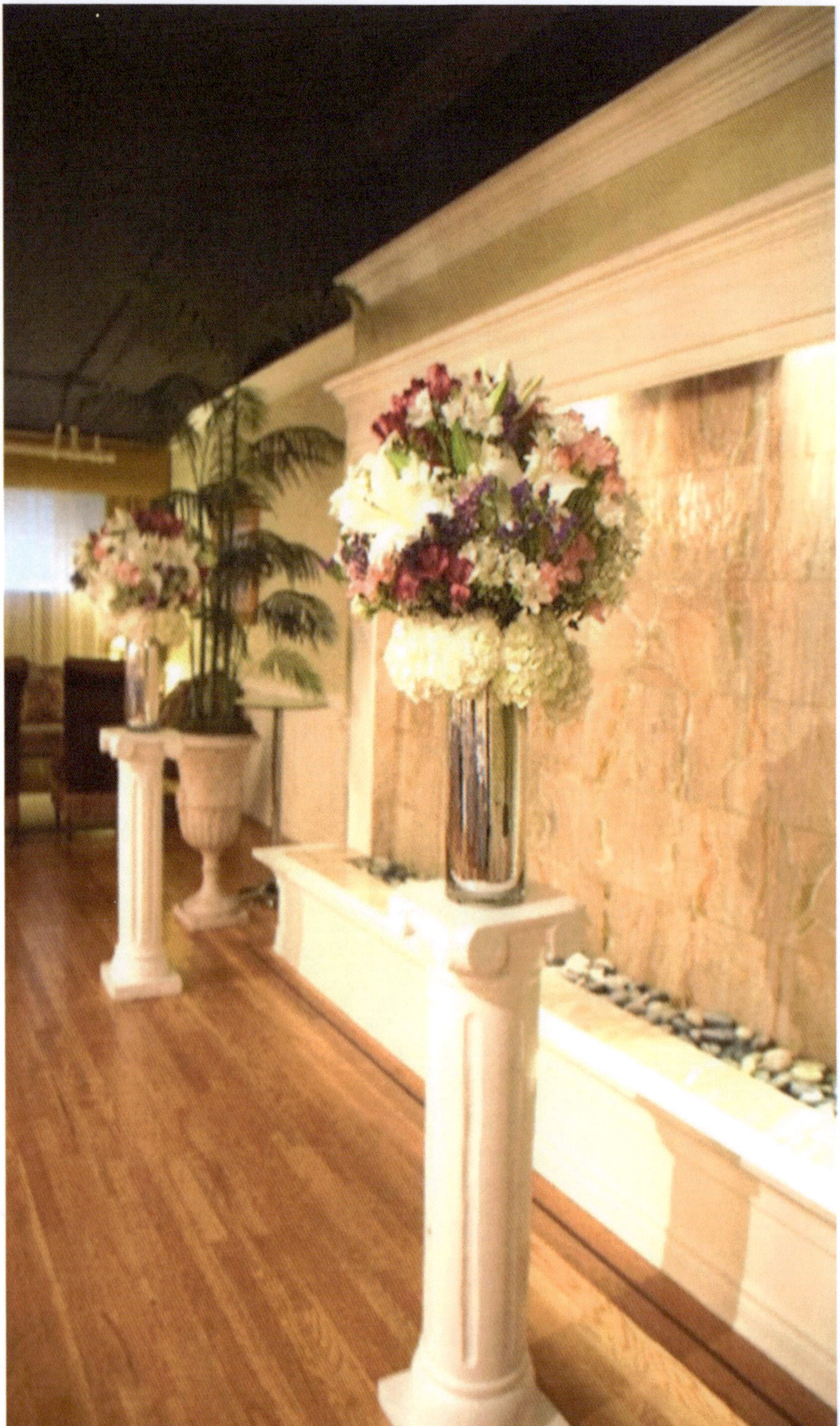

Bouquet-Style Altar Vase Arrangement

This is a larger bouquet-style arrangement in an altar vase. It can be made a couple of days in advance and enjoyed for another 2 weeks afterwards.

MATERIALS:

Tall vase(s), 8-10 hydrangeas, 8-12 fully opened oriental lilies, 8-12 wax flowers, 12-16 spider mums, 12-18 alstromeri, oasis clear tape.

INSTRUCTIONS:

1. Prep your flowers by reading the "Condition Your Flowers" section of this book.
2. Fill the vase with water and flower food. Create a grid pattern with oasis clear tape on the top of the vase.
3. Insert all the wax flowers to create the base layer, then insert other flowers where desired. Be sure to space the flowers accordingly and arrange in a larger pom pom shape. When the final look is achieved, insert the hydrangeas on the inside edge of the vase to frame the flowers. Mist the flowers with water and check the water levels often as hydrangeas drink a lot of water quickly.

See "Care Instructions" section for details on proper care.

4
Centerpieces

Farmers Market Centerpiece

You can make this centerpiece with any flowers from your local farmer's market.

MATERIALS:

Short vase, 6-8 mums, 6-8 assorted dahlias, flower food, oasis clear tape.

INSTRUCTIONS:

1. Prep your flowers by reading the "Condition Your Flowers" section of this book.
2. Fill the vase with water and flower food. Create a grid pattern with oasis clear tape on the top of the vase.
3. Insert all the flowers into the slots in the grid. Be sure to space the flowers accordingly and arrange in a round shape. When the final look is achieved, mist the flowers with water.

See "Care Instructions" section for details on proper care.

Pom Pom Centerpiece

This pom-pom look is achieved by using a smaller vase to give the impression of a free-standing ball of flowers.

MATERIALS:

Short vase, 6-8 overtime, 6-8 orange alstromeri, 8-12 white roses, 8-12 orange gerbera daisies, flower food, oasis clear tape.

INSTRUCTIONS:

1. Prep your flowers by reading the "Condition Your Flowers" section of this book.
2. Fill the vase with water and flower food. Create a grid pattern with oasis clear tape on the top of the vase.
3. Insert all the flowers into the slots in the grid. Be sure to space the flowers accordingly and arrange in a round shape. When the final look is achieved, mist the flowers with water.

See "Care Instructions" section for details on proper care.

5
Planning Your Flowers

~~

It is always a good idea to have a plan of action. This way your wedding flowers will not only be beautiful, but they will fit into the overall design, budget, and logistics of all the components that make up a well-executed life event. After all, this is the big party to kick off your lives together as a married couple. You want it to begin peacefully and have everyone talking for years to come about how much they had enjoyed your wedding.

Guest List

The first thing to consider is your wedding guest list. This guest list is the start to outlining your budget. When considering your budget, you want to think about how your wedding will look in photos. Once your special day has passed, you will only have the memories captured by your wedding pictures. These photos are made extra special with the flowers you fashioned for the wedding party, your marriage ceremony, and the decorations at the reception.

Often, my brides ask me how they can economize and if it is customary to cut back on flowers for family members who are not part of the wedding party, who stand at the altar with the bride and groom. You know your family best and if you think your parents, grandparents, siblings, or any other important people in your family will want a boutonnière or corsage, then add them to the list. Providing flowers for select members of your family and not to others, may be misinterpreted as lack of affection on your part. It is very affordable to have extra boutonnières and corsages made for all in question.

Therefore, it is the best policy is to include everyone in your family, if at all possible. That way the love has been spread around to all in your family and you set a good tone for your family relationships from the wedding onward. You do not want to have an uncaring undertone with any people you are or will become related to. The following checklist is a guideline and will ensure you have considered all who play a part in making your wedding play out like a wonderful movie with you and your new spouse as the main attractions!

Guest and Flowers Checklist

Bride	❏	Bridesmaid(s)	❏
Junior Bridesmaid(s)	❏	Flower Girl(s)	❏
Mother(s)	❏	Grandmother(s)	❏
Groom	❏	Groomsmen	❏
Father(s)	❏	Grandfather(s)	❏
Ring Bearer(s)	❏	Usher(s)	❏
Extended Family	❏	Honored Guest(s)	❏
Officiant	❏	Musician(s)	❏
Altar Arrangements	❏	Aisle Decorations	❏
Centerpieces	❏	Other Items	❏

~ *Budget and Ordering* ~

Your budget is a critical aspect to how much or little you can dedicate to your flowers. Give yourself kudos for not only considering a retail florist, but also doing your flowers yourself. You can do your whole wedding on an affordable budget compared to retail prices if you properly plan for your flowers. It is essential to plan the logistics of the floral portion of the whole event. Otherwise, you could be scrambling at the last minute to get everything together. Do not do that to yourself. Consider these areas when planning your budget and preparing to make your bulk order with your chosen supplier.

DO A DRY RUN BEFORE PRE-ORDERING

It is best to do a dry run on making your bouquet so you can see:
- How long it takes to make a bouquet.
- How many people you need to help you to make these arrangements before the wedding day.
- How many flowers you actually need to pre-order from your local florist.

COST OF FLOWERS

The cost of flowers can vary depending on what kind of flowers you choose to build your wedding flowers with. The number of flowers can also depend on the type of flower you choose.

I often see brides consult about a design that have very expensive non-seasonal flowers. The cost of the materials will skyrocket if you choose special flowers or flowers that are out of season. This is a command issue with celebrity bouquets and featured bouquets in bridal magazines that people come across, but are not familiar with the true cost of such a specialized bouquet. In the end, most people will comment on how beautiful the flowers are and the overall design. You will likely not get people pointing out the specific flower and how special or unseasonal they are. If you are on a budget, then you can supplement out those expensive flowers with seasonal flowers that have a similar size and texture. The overall design can be similar to what you like without breaking the bank.

If you choose standard-sized petal flowers like roses, then you can use these suggested amounts. If you choose large bloomed flowers like a hydrangea, then you can adjust these amounts accordingly. Play with the flowers in your dry run to get a better idea of what you need. Your supplier may ask for your choice of replacement flower if the one you want is out of stock. They may recommend some good options for back-up.

Remember that flowers can grow much larger in warmer seasons or smaller during other seasons, depending on a variety of growing factors at the farms. Being flexible will reduce the stress during the ordering process.

~ *Suggested Amounts for the Pre-Order* ~

Bridal Bouquet	24-40	Flowers
Bridesmaid Bouquet	8-12	Flowers
Flower Girl	4-8	Flowers
Corsages	2-3	Main Flowers
	2-3	Filler Flowers
Boutonnières	1	Main Flowers
	1-2	Filler Flowers
Centerpieces	12	Flowers for a Small
	24	Flowers for a Medium
	36	Flowers for a Large
Altar Arrangements	48-61	Flowers for a Medium
	61-73	Flowers for a Large
Aisle Decorations	6-12	Flowers and fillers

WHERE TO BUY

There are a couple of great places to order flowers. Flower farms and your local grocer are the two main sources for consumers.

Investigate the quality of the flowers and consult with the florist(s) who works there to see if they can fulfill your requirements. You may find some that have a lot of experience working with the public and some with less experience. Some may not even make custom orders for consumers.

Call around and get a consultant to answer your questions about your design and plans before you place your pre-order. Buying from stores that are closer to your home is best so that you do not have far to drive when you need last minute items.

FLOWER FARMS

A great resource to use is local flowers from the flower farms close to you. You can usually pre-order with farmers beforehand.

Each farm will have different requirements for what they need for payment. Half upfront with the rest upon pick-up is common practice.

One thing to keep in mind is that farmers cannot guarantee that your flowers will be the exact color or available when your wedding week arrives. Weather conditions such as excessive rain, a dry season, or any other unforeseen issues will need a back-up plan.

A back-up plan would be to buy your flowers from the grocery store, but you may have to be flexible on your colors and flower choices. What the stores have available is what you have to choose from. If you have to rely on your back-up plan, then shopping at your local grocer or wholesale grocer to buy in bulk are great sources for last minute buys.

GROCERY STORES

Grocery stores are a good place to pre-order your flowers. Many brides are not full-time florists with a business license to buy straight from the wholesale flower distributors, but brides sure can get the same feeling when they pre-order in bulk from their local grocer. Talk to your local florist at your grocery store where you like their flower quality and selection.

Not all grocers are equal when it comes to buying flowers. Like all businesses, grocery chains have different relationships with different flower wholesale houses. They also order in large quantities through industry auctions. Yes, like in commodities trading, flowers are auctioned and traded. Farms participate in these auctions to get the best price for their forecasted stock of flowers. Some grocers buy the freshest flowers in bulk and pass the savings on to their consumers in the form of bouquets at the grocery store.

When you are ready to discuss a large pre-order for your wedding flowers, you can order your flowers made up by the grocery florist, or you can order only the flowers from the florist. Each grocer will have a minimum amount of time for them to place your flower order with their wholesale buyer who will add it onto the store's overall purchase.

Again, there are no guarantees that Mother Nature will produce the exact color and type of flowers you want to pick up. That is why you should consider back-up flowers when certain ones are not available.

~ *Design* ~

When you plan your decorations, the most common two thing brides consider are their colors and a theme. You want to add these two factors into how you design your flowers for your wedding. For example, if your colors are blue, lavender, and ivory, then you want to pick flowers for the season of your wedding. The wedding party flowers, altar and aisle decorations, and the reception flowers are usually designed as an extension of the bridal bouquet. Some brides want everything to match theirs or want them to be designed a little differently with an alternate flower and color combination. Flowers are beautiful accents to the bride and make everything lovely.

See the "bouquets" section of this book for directions of bouquets of previous brides I have consulted for to bring to life their vision of a unique bouquet customized to their personality and personal flare. I hope you will be inspired to come up with your own one-of-a-kind bouquet!

~ *Labor* ~

Often, the execution of a well thought-out plan can fall apart due to lack of accounting for labor. There are many components to planning your wedding where a bride can cut costs by hiring her own friends and family to help pick up supplies and arrange furniture. For making your flowers, I recommend that you do not us anyone who already have a role in the ceremony or have been assigned other tasks. These people already have a lot to do and if you ask them do your flowers too, then they are being spread too thin.

Flowers arrangements are made 1-2 nights before the wedding and your helpers are already doing many things during that time. A bridal bouquet can take up to 1-2 hours to make, which does not include the time to make other flowers. That is why doing a dry run is essential to factoring in what supplies you need and the amount of labor may be involved. Look at your list of helpers and their tasks to see who may be available to help you make the flowers.

After you do a dry run, I recommend that the bride should not be a part of making the flowers so that she is free to do other things and enjoy the final days in the countdown to her big day.

Many brides will be busy entertaining guests who traveled far to attend, actively participating in organizing other responsibilities, attending bridal parties, and do not forget the activities in the rehearsal and dinner that follows. For these reasons, it is best to have someone outside of the wedding party be responsible for making the wedding flowers.

This is the main reason so many brides hire a professional florist to make their flowers for them. Flowers are a great gift to any bride by family members and friends who offer themselves as free labor. Again, once you have identified the people who will take on this responsibility, then do a dry run with them before ordering supplies. Run through the order and make sure they have all they need to fulfill the order, make each item, and are fully equipped with the knowledge and experience to make your floral design.

Having a rough outline of the logistics of labor and execution makes fulfilling your wedding flower orders run smoothly and without worry.

~ *Storage* ~

There are two aspects to consider for storage. You have to store the flowers for making them and you have to store the flowers upon delivering them to the wedding venue on the day of the wedding.

When you pick up your flowers from the store a day or two before hand, you will need to clean them and store them in a "cool" place in your house. A cold basement or ground level of the house is good places to store the stock flowers. Keep in mind that flowers will continue to bloom in "cool" areas as well. This is a trick to get that full bloomed look from your flowers instead of all the flowers being closed on the wedding day.

Some flowers may need longer than 1-2 days to bloom. During the dry run you can see identify which ones you need more time to bloom. Oriental lilies are great examples of taking a little longer to bloom. You may have to store such flowers longer than the other flowers in your arrangement. Factor these into your storage plan.

An extra refrigerator is a bonus, or reserved some space in another refrigerator for the flowers. Keep the temperature between 40 and 72 degrees Fahrenheit (18 to 22 degrees Celsius).

A storage room or garage at a "cool", not freezing, temperature for the bouquets and cut flowers, such as the centerpieces is fine as they are in water in the vases. They will open up a little over night and fully opened for the next day.

Be sure to double check that the room temperature is not too warm. A room temperature between 40 and 72 degrees should be fine. Really warm rooms will wilt the flowers and really cold rooms will freeze them.

Most flowers are best displayed away from direct sunlight, heating or cooling vents, directly under ceiling fans, or on top of televisions or radiators, which give off heat and can cause flowers to dehydrate.

Avoid placing fresh flowers near ripening fruit, which releases tiny amounts of ethylene gas that can age them prematurely.

You can store the corsages and boutonnières in the fridge as they do not sit in water. Boutonnières and corsages are best made the night before and kept fresh in the fridge until they are ready to adorn on the wedding party on the wedding day.

~ *Conditioning Your Flowers* ~

There are two things you do to condition your flowers before you begin your bouquets and flower arrangements. Put them in fresh water that has flower food and strip them of stems and unwanted leaves. Take the flowers out of the packaging and immediately put them in buckets of fresh cool water that has the appropriate amount of flower food. If you bought the flowers from the store, then the florist should supply you with the right amount of flower food for the amount of flowers. Otherwise, I recommend buying some flower food at the local hardware store in the floral department or floral shop. They should have the amounts you need to buy.

Once the flowers are in water, then you need to begin removing the leaves and thorns from each flower. For roses, you can avoid removing thorns by selecting roses that do not grow thorns or making sure the thorns are removed by the store. If you want to have some leaves at the top of flowers, then strip off the rest of the leaves and leave the top ones for design purposes. Removing the leaves allows the flower to drink as much of the water as possible without having the water replenish the leaves on the way up to the head of the flower. Cut 1-2 inches from the bottom of the stem that has likely dried out before putting the stem back into the water.

Now you have fresh flowers that are not distressed from the trip from the farm to your house. Allow 1-3 days depending on the flower to reach the bloom size you prefer before using them to make your bouquets and flower arrangements.

~ *Delivery* ~

If you choose to purchase flowers from a retail florist, ask them if they deliver and what their delivery costs are. Some florists will deliver your order to the facility, but they will charge for the delivery so factor in the mileage costs. Add the expected delivery cost to your overall order to make sure it falls within your budget. Other florists do not deliver, because they do not want to risk damaging your flowers during the delivery.

Whether you are picking up your flowers from the store or from someone's house, you will need a delivery plan. It is best to plan on having the right type of transportation for your flowers. A minivan or a rental truck is often great choices – and they aren't too expensive to rent for a day.

If your flowers are too large for the car you plan on using, then I would recommend renting a small commercial truck or full size van to haul them.

As for supporting the flowers in the van to prevent them from tipping over and breaking, consider using cardboard boxes in appropriate sizes. You can get cardboard boxes that are shorter in height by calling stores and asking them if you can pick up their boxes before they dispose of them. Often, stores will get new shipments during the night and dispose of boxes before the day shift begins. If you call the store manager and request boxes that fit the height limit you need to fit your bouquet vases in, then they may reserve some for you. You can also buy boxes at local retailers that sell packaging materials.

When you get your boxes, then just cut an "X" that fits the base size of your vases and stick the vases into the snug cut-out. A snug fit of the bouquet vases should transport your flowers safely to the wedding venue.

I suggest you have a customized holder made with wood for transporting larger flowers - such as altar arrangements, to prevent them from tipping over during delivery due to their heavy weight. You can build a solid base so it cannot tip over with some supports for the vase. This way, they are secure for transport.

Do a dry run with the vases filled with water and the flowers in the holders to give you the best idea of what to expect.

You might have to make 2 separate deliveries: one delivery for the ceremony arrangements and one for the reception flowers. You will deliver the ceremony flowers to where the ceremony will be held. If the ceremony is held at a separate facility from where the reception will be held, then I recommend delivering them to the ceremony facility and making sure that they have a refrigerator to store the bouquets, the boutonnières and corsages.

The altar arrangements and aisle decorations will be delivered and stored at the ceremony location, but then you will need to transport them to the reception location if you plan on re-using them for the reception.

Reception centerpieces will have to be delivered and stored at the reception location. Pay special attention to the room temperatures of the ceremonial area and where the reception will be held. Some facilities will automatically turn up the room temperature, which can wilt your flowers. If applicable, talk to the building manager to ensure the right temperature is maintained for your flowers.

Once the festivities take place, the room will warm up a little from the people inside it. If the ceremony is outside, then deliver the flowers to a room that is "cool" in temperature until 30 minutes to 1 hour before the ceremony begins. Then move them to the outside places they will be displayed at. This will keep them fresh longer. This alternative plan is great if it is hot outside.

~ *Set-up* ~

Set-up is primarily for the altar flowers, aisle decorations, and reception flowers. Take care in factoring the total weight of the altar flowers including the vase weight and the weight of the flowers in the water. A dry run will give you a good idea of how stable it will be.

If you plan on having the altar flowers sit on the ground, then make sure the ground is solid and stable.

If you plan on having them on grass, then make sure the ground is not soggy and that it will not sink in. Unstable ground will tip the flowers over and break them.

If you are placing your altar flowers on a podium, then do a dry run with the flowers on the podium you are using. Remember, the altar flowers are top heavy. Make sure the base is sturdy and heavy enough to hold the altar flowers on safely without tipping over. Again, ensure that the ground is solid.

For reception flowers, remember the flowers need to be in a cool place so they do not wilt in the sun or a hot room. You can go ahead and place the reception flowers on the tables if the room is cool. Sun shining on the flowers on the tables is fine as long as the room is not too warm. If you are unsure, then do a dry run to alleviate concerns with set-up.

There are no set-up for bouquets, boutonnières, and corsages. They go from the fridge and cool storage area to the wedding party.

6
Care Instructions For Flowers

~~~

Please read these instructions carefully to ensure the best care for your flowers.

BOUTONNIERES AND CORSAGES

A fridge can store the corsages and boutonnières as they do not sit in water. They just need to be at a "cool" temperature, between 34 and 36 degrees Fahrenheit.

PINNING INSTRUCTIONS

Place the boutonnière or pin the corsage on your outfit where you want it to be pinned, then pick (pinch) a piece of the fabric.

Be sure to slide the pin up through the fabric and up into the meatiest, thickest part of the stem or flower. The pin should rest right in the center of the flower. This will secure it from pricking the wearer. You should only need one pin, but a second one should be available if needed for boutonnières. Pinned corsages will use two pins.

BOUQUETS AND CUT FLOWERS

Store enough water with flower food in the vase to give the flowers water to drink, but do not fill with water past the height of the decorations to prevent them from getting soaked.

Do not forget to mist the flowers with a spray bottle to refresh them. You can mist them with a spray bottle every day until the wedding day. If the flowers look a touch dry and it has been a little while between mistings, then you can mist them again, but be careful not to over mist them to the point they are dripping with water.

Store them in a storage room or garage at a "cool", not freezing, temperature for the bouquets and cut flowers, such as the centerpieces, is fine as they are in water in the vases. They will open up a little over night and be full for the next day.

CARE/STORAGE RECAP

The care and storage of flowers is so important for their freshness on your wedding day that I repeat it here:

- Double-check that the **room temperature** is moderate (not warm). Really warm rooms will wilt the flowers and really cold rooms will freeze them.
- Most flowers prefer temperatures between **65 to 72 degrees Fahrenheit** (18 to 22 degrees Celsius).
- Keep the flowers away from direct **sunlight**, **heating**, or **cooling** vents, directly under **ceiling fans**, or on top of **televisions** or **radiators** (which give off heat so could cause the flowers to dehydrate).
- Avoid placing fresh flowers near ripening **fruit**, which releases tiny amounts of ethylene gas that can age them prematurely.

7
Wedding Day Timeline

Aside from my experience with making flowers for my brides, I often get requests for tips on making their wedding day perfect and am asked to provide any suggestions they may have not considered. Let's look at planning your timeline so that the beautiful flowers you made for your wedding is enjoyed by everyone all through the festivities.

Have you ever wondered why weddings often run so far behind the scheduled time, but everyone had been running around frantically to get things moving along? Well, it is because the wedding did not have a solid timeline that factored everything in or the wedding planner did not keep everyone to schedule.

Everyone is familiar with a wedding planner checklist for many months up to the wedding day, but sometimes people forget to draft out a very critical wedding-day timeline. This will ensure that operations run smoothly, preventing your guests from sitting a long time waiting for the ceremony to begin and to ensure that the photo-taking, ceremony, cocktail hour, reception, and clean-up activities run on time.

My first recommendation is to have a designated person who does not have a task already to look after this task. Do not even think about having the bride or groom as the wedding planner. It is your wedding day and the bride and groom should be able to enjoy the day instead of taking on the responsibility of being the point person for these tasks.

The wedding planner's job is to follow the timeline that was drafted up. They keep the wedding party from taking too long to get ready, and keep them on track so they make it to the ceremony and reception location within the time allotted. The planner is the point person to help the florist, caterers, and other staff when they need to know where to put things and where things are at the venue. This person is also the contact person you put on the wedding announcements for your guest to call if they are lost or if there are last minute cancellations. As you can see, it is best not to assign this role to someone actively taking part in the wedding. Depending on the responsibilities of a groomsman or a bridesmaid, you may be able to assign this role to one of them.

In terms of planning your timeline, I would begin by talking non-attendance. The average turnover for last minute cancellations from my previous clients who experience this is 10-15%. That means you could likely experience that 10-15% of your guests who RSVP will not be able to make it to the wedding due to unforeseen circumstances, such as being able to find a babysitter or a problem with transportation.

You cannot guarantee that everyone will make it, but you can try to compensate for possible non-attendance by sending a friendly reminder at least two weeks prior to the wedding day. This informal reminder sent via email, text message, or as a post-it on your wedding website, should inform them that you are looking forward to seeing them at the wedding.

If there is a possibility that they may get lost, provide the point person's contact information. List any friendly reminders that are critical for the guests, such as allocated parking, etc.

Lastly, write in the reminder that if for any reason, they may not be able to attend, that they let you know and that you understand that unforeseen things can happen. What is frustrating to the bride and groom is that regardless if everyone attends or not, the wedding has been paid for already. Therefore, mon-attendance is a waste of money. Sending out a friendly reminder a little ahead of time will let your guests know that you have no hard feelings if they may not be able to attend, and remind them of the times of all the activities so they do not forget.

You would be surprised how many people unintentionally forget the wedding date and time. You may now be able to invite people you wanted to invite, but could not due to lack of space. So your fitness trainer, nanny, co-workers you worked with for years can be invited at last minute when new slots become open.

Many people understand that they might not get an invitation due to lack of space and that close friends and primary family must be invited first.

In planning your wedding-day timeline, begin with all the activities and time it takes to get to the venue backwards from the ceremony. From the ceremony time, plan all the way back to when the bride gets up in the morning to get ready. Then from the ceremony time, plan forward through the wedding festivities all the way to what time to begin breaking down the tables and chairs to close out the facility. Here is a rough guideline for you to work from when planning your own wedding day timeline.

This is an hour-by-hour guide to the day's post ceremonial events. Do not forget to email guests reminders at least 2 weeks before for last minute changes and updates. The wedding countdown is on!

~ *Wedding-Day Timeline Example* ~

7:00-11:00	Eat breakfast and get ready
10:00-2:00	Set-up reception tables, ceremony decorations, catering, flowers, cake set-up, and sound system
12:00	Wedding party arrives. Boutonnières are pinned on families as they arrive
12:00-2:30	Bride and Groom, wedding-party and family photos
2:30-3:15	Play ceremony prelude music and wedding-party waits in back rooms
2:50-3:20	Ushers hand out programs to guests
3:30-4:00	Ceremony
4:00-4:45	Cocktails (play cocktail music and caterer serves the newlyweds in the backroom before they're announced)
4:45-5:30	Dinner announced (caterer serves the newlyweds at the head table before they greet guests)
5:30-6:00	Toast and cake
6:00-6:15	First dance, followed by other pairings
6:15-7:30	Bouquet toss and open dance floor
7:15-7:30	Last call for the bar and last dance
7:45-9:30	Farewell at the parking lot, pack-up, and give keys to facility manager

Other lists to consider are:
- ➢ Rainy Day Alternative Timeline
- ➢ Inventory Check List
- ➢ Vendors Contact List

8
Salutations

Marriage is a commitment you and your spouse make to nurture that special bond you have as you grow old together. As you have read, if you choose to make your own flowers for your wedding, there is a lot of pre-planning involved to have a smooth operation. You cannot plan everything as small issues can surface, but many brides work with their friends and family to find creative solutions to problems that can arise with their flowers.

An open and actively supporting attitude is critical to any partnership. Planning your flowers requires support and communication without drama. This is a good foundation for the beginning of your marital relationship. Although a lot of work and planning have been made to ensuring your wedding day is beautiful and the bride and the groom enjoy it, remember that the wedding day is just a ***day***. Marriage is a journey. You will have planned the flowers for your wedding to be beautiful and you will have executed it well so you can enjoy your special day as the first fruit of a well-prepared planting season.

Your marriage is filled with the seeding of love and tender care is needed to play out a relationship full of the fruits of your successes together.

Yes, there will likely be bumps on the road, but open communication and active participation to adapt and problem-solve together will help ensure your marriage is joyous when you look back at your life and think of your union from the wedding day forward.

About the Author

Von D. Galt is a self-taught wedding florist in Seattle, WA, USA. She began her floral arrangement hobby creating custom bridal bouquets for friends and family before offering it to the public in her wedding flower business. In *"Bridal Bouquets: Tips to Design Your Own Wedding Flowers"*, readers get instruction for how to create custom wedding flowers specific to the unique tastes of the bride herself. Von earned her Bachelor of Arts degree from the University of Washington and earned her MBA in E-Business Management from Westwood College of Technology.

Index

A

accent ....vi, 35
aisle decorations..71, 74, 77, 82, 83
alstromeria. 3, 17, 27, 30, 36, 38, 42, 45, 47, 49, 56, 63, 66, 75, 79
Alstromeria, Carnation, & Wax Flowers................................... 57
altar flowers.................................. 83
arrangements 72, 74, 77, 80, 81, 82
attitude 93
auctions 76

B

back-up plan 75
bloom size...................................... 81
bouquet holder....47, 49, 51, 53, 55
Bouquets:
  Amour Duree de Vie Bouquet... 53
  Baroque Remembrance Bouquet.................................. 43
  Beach Romance Bouquet.......... 23
  Blush Pink Bouquet............ 21, 51
  Bouquet Style Altar Vase............65
    Arrangement 74
  Daffodils in Spring Bouquet 47
  Dainty Delights Bouquet 39
  Early Spring Bouquet 31
  Extraordinarily Unique Bouquet.................................. 45
  First Crush Bouquet 11
  Friendship First Bouquet........... 27
  Happy Delights Bouquet 3
  Happy Flowers Bouquet............ 41
  Nous Nous Marions Bouquet....55
  Pearly White Bouquet................. 5
  Plum Accents Bouquet.............. 35
  Purple and Ivory Roses Bouquet.................................. 17
  Rock of Love Bouquet 15
  Romance of the Sea Bouquet.................................. 13
  Rouge Bisou Bouquet................ 49
  Scholarly Musings Bouquet....... 25
  Spring Breeze Bouquet.............. 33
  Sunflower and Friends Bouquet..9
  Three Tiers Bouquet.................... 7
  Uniquely Yours Bouquet 37
  Victorian Ambiance Bouquet.................................. 19
  Year Round Flowers Bouquet.................................. 29
boutonniere(s).....iv, 69, 59, 70, 74, 80, 82, 84, 85, 86, 92
bow 9, 13, 58, 59, 60
boxes..................................... 81, 82
brooch................... 11, 19, 23, 41
budget.............iv, 69, 70, 72, 73, 81
bulk 72, 76

C

cancellations 89

carnations. 5, 13, 15, 23, 39, 41, 43, 45, 47, 51, 53, 58, 59
cascading. 47, 49, 51, 53, 55
Centerpieces:
　Farmers Market Centerpiece.... 67
　Pom Pom Centerpiece 68
ceremony . v, 70, 77, 82, 83, 89, 91, 92
chrysanthemums....3, 5, 13, 27, 54, 63, 73, 75, 78
clean-up.. 89
clear tape 63, 65, 67, 68
cocktail 89, 91, 92
color 11, 17, 75, 76, 77
corsage pins...........3, 5, 7, 9, 11, 13, 15,17, 19, 21, 23, 25, 27, 29, 31, 33, 35, 37, 39, 41, 43, 45, 57, 58, 59, 60
corsages iv,v, 56, 57, 58, 70, 74, 80, 82, 84, 85, 86
cost............................72, 73, 77, 81
countdown 78, 91
customized holder...................... 82

D

daffodils....................................... 47
dahlias 67
daisies.................. 3, 5, 7, 31, 41, 68
delivery.............................. iv, 81, 82
distributors................................. 76
dry run.vi, 72, 73, 78, 79, 82, 83, 84
dusty miller........................ 19,21,35

F

farmer's market.......................... 67
ferns 53
floral adhesive 59, 60
floral tape. 3, 5, 7, 9, 11, 13, 15, 17, 19, 21, 23, 25, 27, 29, 31, 33, 35, 37, 39, 41, 43, 45, 57, 58, 59, 60
flower farms 75
flower food....63, 65, 67, 68, 80, 86
freesias 5, 21, 27, 33, 35, 39, 45
fresh 76, 80, 81, 83,87
fridge 80, 84, 85
fruit................................. 80, 87, 94

G

gerbera daisy 49
gladiolas................................ 59, 73
grass 15, 83
grid 63, 65, 67, 68
grocery store 75,76
guest list 70

H

hardware store 80
heather flowers 45
hot glue gun....7, 15, 39, 47, 49, 51, 53, 55
hydrangeas 31, 33, 41, 63, 65
hypericum berries 19

I

invitation 91

J

Japanese fatsias 63

L

last minute buys 76
leaves 33, 47, 53, 63, 80
lilies:....5, 7, 11, 23, 27, 29, 35, 41, 47, 51, 53, 63, 65, 79
   Asiatic 11, 29, 41, 47
   Calla 35, 45
   Oriental. 7, 23, 27, 51, 53, 63, 65, 79
location 82, 89

M

mist 63, 65, 67, 68, 86
monte casinos 47
morning 91

O

oasis 59, 60, 63, 65, 67, 68
orchids 39
out of season 73
overtime .. 21, 23, 31, 35, 51, 63, 68

P

packaging 80, 82
pearl shoots 13, 43, 59
pearl strands 5, 23

poms 7, 15, 27
pre-order 72, 74, 75, 76
pre-plan .... vi, 93
problem-solve 94
pruning shears 3, 5, 7, 9, 11, 13, 15, 17, 19, 21, 23, 25, 27, 29, 31, 33, 35, 37, 39, 41, 43, 45, 47, 49, 51, 53, 55, 57, 58

R

reception....v, 70, 77, 82, 83, 89, 92
reminder 90, 91
retail florist 72, 81
rhinestones 7, 39
ribbon. .3, 5, 7, 9, 11, 13, 15, 17, 19, 21, 23, 25, 27, 29, 31, 33, 35, 37, 39, 41, 43, 47, 49, 51, 53, 55, 59, 60
Rose, Carnation, and Wax Flowers 58
Rose, Mini Carnation, and Ribbon 59
roses 9, 11, 13, 15, 17, 19, 21, 23, 25, 27, 29, 31, 37, 43, 49, 51, 53, 58, 68, 73, 80
RSVP 90

S

Safety Alert........3, 5, 7, 9, 11, 13, 15, 17, 19, 21, 23, 25, 27, 29, 31, 33, 35, 37, 39, 41, 43, 45, 57, 58, 59, 60

saran wrap........... 47, 49, 51, 53, 55
satin... 3, 5, 7, 13, 15,17, 19, 21, 23, 25, 27, 29,31, 33, 35, 37, 39, 43
seasonal flowers...............41, 72, 73
set-up 83,84,92
shearers.....................66, 67, 68, 69
Sprayed Out Altar Vase 69
   Arrangement .61,63,65,71,73,74,77,79,80,81, 82
sprengeri ferns 53
stem adhesive spray.47, 49, 51, 53, 55
stems 3, 5, 7,9,11, 13, 15, 17, 19, 21, 23, 25, 27,29, 31, 33, 35, 37, 39,41, 43, 45, 57, 58, 63,80
stock ... 9, 25, 35, 43, 45, 49, 60, 73, 76,79
stock flowers ... 9, 43, 45, 49, 60, 79
storage room........................79, 86
sunflowers 9

T

temperature(s) 79, 82, 83, 85,86,87
theme 77
thistle 37, 43
thorns 80
timeline 88, 89, 90,91,92
top heavy.................................... 83
transport(ation)................81, 82, 90
two tone 51

U

unforeseen circumstances.......... 90

V

vase .47, 49, 51, 53,55, 63,65,67,68 79, 82, 83, 86
velvet...................47, 49, 51, 53, 55
venue..................... v, 79, 82, 89, 91

W

water.47, 49, 51, 53, 55, 63, 65, 67, 68, 79, 80, 81, 82, 83,85,86
wax flowers 7, 13,15, 19, 49, 57, 58, 65
wedding party.... v,vi,70, 77, 78, 80, 84, 89, 92
wedding planner......................... 89
weight.................................. 82, 83
white static 9
wholesale 76
wrist bracelets 59, 60
wrist corsage 5, 59, 60
weather 75

Y

year round 29

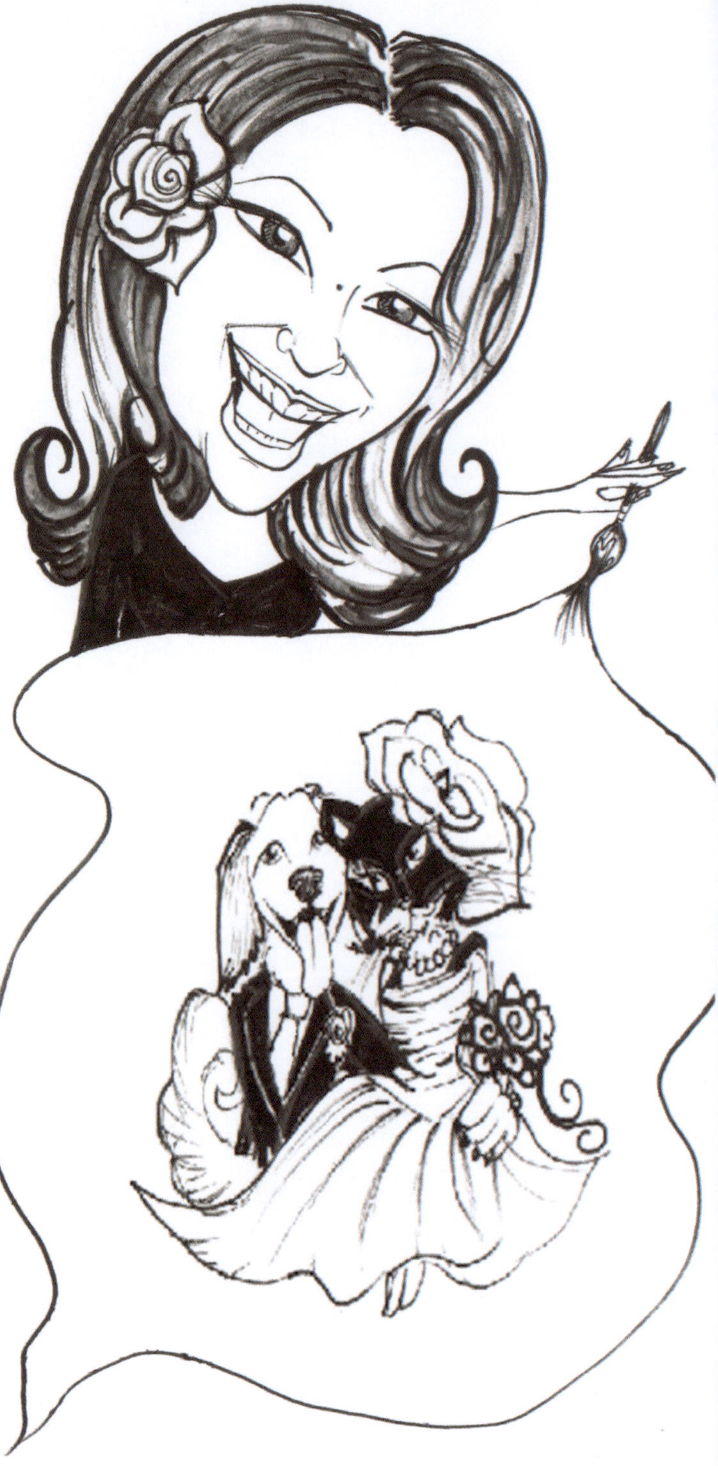

Printed in Great Britain
by Amazon